1　富士曼荼羅図　16世紀

"Fuji Mandala," 16th c.

2 紅白梅図屛風　尾形光琳筆　18世紀

"Red and White Plum Blossoms," by Ogata Korin, 18th c.

3 山越阿弥陀図 13世紀
"Amitabha Crossing the Mountains," 13th c.

4 富嶽三十六景のうち神奈川沖浪裏　葛飾北斎筆　19世紀
"Fuji through the Waves," by Katsushika Hokusai, 19th c.

5　高雄観楓図　狩野秀頼筆　16世紀

"Maple Viewing at Takao," by Kano Hideyori, 16th c.

6 凍雲篩雪図　浦上玉堂筆　19世紀

"Landscape in Snow," by Uragami Gyokudo, 19th c.

7 獅子頭をかぶって踊る人

Men dancing in the guise of a lion

著者まえがき

　日本人が抱く心情や美意識は、何に由来しているのだろうか――その私なりの答えをできるだけわかりやすく記したのが本書である。

　結論から先に言ってしまうと、かつて川端康成(かわばたやすなり)氏もノーベル賞の受賞に際し語っている「雪月花(せつげつか)」という句に託された、「自然や四季のめぐりとの交流」という考え方に尽きる。

　そこで、代表的な神仏の造型、詩歌(しいか)、文芸、禅、建築、美術などを辿ることで、そうした考え方へ至る根本の道筋を明らかにすることにした。

　本書は、同名の単行本を再出版したものである。図版の一部を差し替えたが、本文は当初のまま変えていない。初版から21年、思うに世界の状勢は変わったが、日本人の心情や美意識に大きな変化はあるまい。

　いま、この本とはじめて出会う若い人たちがどのように読み、反応してくれるのかを楽しみにしている。

2008年10月吉日

　　　　　　　　　　　　　　　　　　　　　　　栗田勇

Author's Preface

In this book I recorded, in the easiest-to-understand terms, my response to the question of where the sensibilities and sense of beauty of the Japanese come from.

My conclusion is that they derive entirely from communion with nature and the cycle of the four seasons, summed up in the phrase *setsu-getsu-ka*—"snow, moon and flowers."

What I thus aimed for was to shed light on the fundamental path to this way of thinking by tracing representative Shinto and Buddhist forms, native poetry and literature, Zen philosophy, local architecture and art, etc.

The present volume is a new format of a work originally published under the same title in 1987. Although some of the earlier illustrations have been replaced here, the original text is retained. The world has changed significantly in the 21 years since the book's initial release, but I believe that the sensibilities and sense of beauty of the Japanese people have changed little in the intervening years.

I look forward to seeing how today's young people, reading this book for the first time, will interpret and react to it.

Isamu Kurita

October 2008

ごあいさつ

　本書は、富士通グループの外国人経営者を対象としたセミナーで行われた栗田先生のご講演内容をもとに、先生のご好意により一冊の本にまとめたものです。

　初版発刊後21年が経過し、グローバル化の進展と共に日本が世界の多種多様な文化と深いかかわりを持つ機会が増しています。そのような時にこそ、我々日本人が日本文化および日本人の精神の本質を再認識し、確固たる基軸をもって行動することが求められてきております。

　このような時代背景のもと、日本文化の本質が簡潔明瞭に和英対訳で述べられている本書が、このたび新書版として復刻されましたことは、当社にとって大変光栄なことと存じます。

　本書が読者の皆様の日本文化理解の手引書として異文化の交流に少しでもお役に立ちましたら、誠に幸いに存じます。

2008年10月吉日

　　　　　　　　　　株式会社FUJITSUユニバーシティ
　　　　　　　　　　代表取締役会長　斑目廣哉

Foreword

This book is based on a lecture delivered by Professor Isamu Kurita at a seminar for foreign management staff of Fujitsu Group companies during the 1980s. It was originally compiled into book form in 1987, together with an English translation, with Professor Kurita's generous permission.

Twenty-one years have passed since this work's first printing, and in the interim Japan, amid the sweep of globalization, has had increasing occasions to engage closely with diverse cultures from around the world. It is precisely in times like these that we Japanese are called on to recognize anew the essence both of our native culture and of our identity as Japanese, so that they may serve as the foundation of our actions.

In response to these needs, we take pride in reprinting, in a new format, Professor Kurita's book concisely and lucidly describing the essence of Japanese culture for both native and foreign readers. We hope that as an introduction to understanding Japanese culture, it will prove beneficial to the promotion of intercultural exchanges.

Hiroya Madarame
Chairman, FUJITSU University

October 2008

雪月花の心───── **目次**

Ⅰ. 序──日本文化の特質「雪月花」 20
- 日本文化のキーワード 24
- 古代と現在の共存 26
- 日本人の自然観 32
- 空間の演出 40

Ⅱ. 詩文学に表わされた日本人の心情 42
- 和歌と俳句 42
- 聖フランチェスコと明恵上人(みょうえ) 44
- 桜の下で死を希(ねが)った西行(さいぎょう)法師 50
- 雪月花と一体化 64
- 「座(ざ)」の文学 66

Ⅲ. 図版で見る日本人の心と形 70
1. 日本の歴史を概観 70
- 縄文文化と弥生文化 71
- 仏教伝来と伝統文化 72
- 鎖国(さこく)の歴史的評価 76
- 天皇について 84

2. 古代の世界(飛鳥・奈良・平安時代) 88
- 神道の神殿 88
- 伊勢神宮と出雲大社 92
- 法隆寺(ほうりゅうじ)・五重の塔 96
- 凍(こお)れる音楽 108

Japanese Identity ———— Contents

I. Introduction —— *Setsu-Getsu-Ka* 21
- A symbolic phrase 25
- Ancient sensibilities 27
- The Japanese concept of nature 33
- Interior space 39

II. The Japanese Heart as Experience in Poetry 43
- Haiku and *Waka* 43
- The St. Francis of Japan 45
- A poem prophesying one's death 51
- Reaching oneness with nature 65
- Linked verse 67

III. The Japanese Mind and Form 71
1. Overview of Japanese History 71
- The Jomon and Yayoi cultures 71
- The introduction of Buddhism 72
- Effects of national seclusion 77
- The Japanese imperial system 85

2. The Ancient Period (Asuka, Nara, Heian) 89
- Ise Shrine 89
- Izumo Shrine 93
- The five-storied pagoda 97
- Frozen music 109

菩薩の表現　108
　　地上の極楽浄土　112
　　『源氏物語』の世界　124
　3．中世の世界（鎌倉・室町・桃山時代）　136
　　日本の肖像画　136
　　金閣と銀閣　144
　　「枯山水」　152
　　墨絵の三大特徴　164
　　日本間の装飾美術　168
　　茶の湯と利休　168
　4．近世の世界（江戸時代）　178
　　日光・東照宮　178
　　桂離宮の庭園　182
　　遊女の風俗と生活　184
　　歌麿の女性表現　186

Ⅳ．結び――現代に生きる〈茶の湯〉の精神　190
　　茶室への招待　192
　　「一期一会」　194
　　日本人の倫理性　198
　　「潔い」ということ　200
　　雪月花の風景　214

　　図版掲載作品・解説　216

The bodhisattva　109
　　　An earthly paradise　113
　　　The Tale of Genji　125
　3. The Middle Ages (Kamakura, Muromachi, Momoyama)　137
　　　Japanese portraiture　137
　　　Golden and Silver Pavilions　145
　　　Dry landscapes　153
　　　Japanese ink paintings　165
　　　Sliding panel decorations　169
　　　The teahouse　169
　4. The Modern Period (Edo)　179
　　　Toshogu Shrine　179
　　　Garden of Katsura　183
　　　The demimonde　185
　　　A portrait by Utamaro　187

Ⅳ. Conclusion──
　The Tea Ceremony Spirit　191
　　　The path to the teahouse　193
　　　The phrase "ichigo-ichie"　195
　　　Japanese morality　199
　　　The foremost criterion　201
　　　The view of "setsu-getsu-ka"　215

　　　Detailed descriptions of all figures　217

注意
1．図版番号のうち、白抜き数字（例：**1**）は、それについて本文中で言及されている作品であることを示す。そうでないもの（例：3）は、本文中では直接触れていないが、関連作品であることを示す。
2．収録図版の作品解説は、巻末216〜243ページに掲載した。

NOTES
1. Figures designated by boxed numbers (eg. **1**) are referred to in the text. Figures with plain numbers (eg.3), though not directly mentioned, are given as additional references.
2. Detailed descriptions of all figures are found on pages 217-243.
3. With the exception of persons of the modern period (post-1868), Japanese names are rendered in English according to the original Japanese order, i.e. surname preceding given name.

雪月花の心
せつ げつ か
Japanese Identity

栗田 勇
英訳 ロバート・ミンツァー
企画 FUJITSU ユニバーシティ

Isamu Kurita
Robert A. Mintzer
FUJITSU University

祥伝社新書
Shodensha Shinsho

Ⅰ．序─日本文化の特質「雪月花」

▶**クロスカルチャーとは**　遠く海外から、みなさんをお迎えし、日本についてお話しする機会を得たことを、たいへんうれしく思います。最近、とりわけ経済の見地から日本式経営であるとか、日本論というようなものが、雑誌、新聞などでさかんに採（と）り上げられていて、流行になっている観すらあります。

　今回は少し見地を変えて、直接に経営論とは結びつきませんが、これからの世界的なビジネスにも必須のテーマであり、特に富士通（ふじつう）のモットーであるところの"クロスカルチャー"という見地から「日本人とその文化」の問題を考えてみたいと思います。

　すでに、みなさんは来日して、能、狂言、歌舞伎をご覧になりました。

　能は、はじめのうちは、なかなかわかりにくく退屈に見えますが、深みがあります。一方、歌舞伎は、西欧でいえば一種のオペラのようなもので、日本の中流や上流の階層では、家族で、あるいは恋人などと一緒に、歌舞伎見物に行くことをたいへん楽しみにしております。また会社の招待にもよく用いられています。

　もちろん、今日の日本人は、歌舞伎の中の侍と同じではありません。日本人は、それほど特殊でもなく、かといって、まったく西欧人と共通でもありません。

I. **INTRODUCTION**——*Setsu-Getsu-Ka*

▶**What is "cross-culture"?** It is a great pleasure to be given this opportunity to speak about Japan to our guests from overseas.

In recent times many articles have appeared in the printed media concerning Japan and its management practices, almost to the extent of becoming a fad.

Today, therefore, I will not speak specifically about Japanese management but instead will turn my attention to a topic destined to assume paramount importance in conducting business on global scale in the future: the special character of the Japanese and their culture. This topic is especially apt since it relates so closely to one of Fujitsu's principal themes, namely, cross-cultural cooperation.

I understand that you have already seen a presentation of Kabuki. Kabuki is generally said to be more interesting than Noh, which tends to bore first-time audiences because it is rather difficult to understand.

In contrast, Kabuki in some ways corresponds to opera in the West, and the middle and upper levels of Japanese society take great enjoyment in going to Kabuki as a family entertainment or as a venue for dating. Japanese companies also frequently invite their important guests to Kabuki performances.

Modern Japanese people, of course, are quite different from the samurai who appear in a Kabuki play. They are by no means as "special in character" as the samurai. And yet, modern Japanese are not exactly identical to their Western counterparts either.

▶異文化理解のために　ところで、日本の文化と言いましても、日本人自身がいつも自覚しているわけではありません。なぜなら、文化というものはひじょうに多くの要素の複合体であり、目に見えるもののほかに、歴史、伝統など目に見えないものもたくさん含んでいるからです。そのうえ、ふだんは気づかないものでありながら、それでいて、あるとき理屈を超えて表面に現われてくるものです。

　たとえば貿易摩擦の問題にしても、すでに論理と数字の問題を超えて、感情的な面が出てきているというのも、やはり文化ギャップというものが原因でしょう。そういう意味でも、文化の相互理解というものは、生活や政治・経済のより深い理解のためにも欠くべからざるものです。

　しかし、とは言いましても、文化の交流ということは、けっして、文化の同面性、あるいは共通性だけを理解するということではありません。むしろ、それぞれの個々の文化の特殊性や違う点を、認識、理解するということによって、はじめて共同作業と友情が生まれます。それがひいては、経済的にも生産性を高め、世界を豊かにすることにつながるものであります。

　そもそも、互いに相異のあるということが、つねに共感を妨(さまた)げるものではありません。それなら男性と女性が愛しあうことはできないはずです。東洋では、陽(いん)と陰(よう)とは和合(わごう)を前提とした対比のプロセスと考え、男と女

▶ **A cultural gap** "Japanese culture," naturally, is not something which the Japanese themselves are conscious of at all times. This is because culture itself is a complex fusion of an extremely large number of elements, including many which are not visible or tangible, such as history and tradition. Nevertheless, culture does become apparent at certain times as a manifestation of social aspects which transcend logic.

The trade imbalance, for example, has become a subject which today exceeds mere questions of numbers and logic. Today it is also fraught with various emotional factors which, inherently, are tied to a basic cultural gap.

In this respect, an understanding of culture is indispensable to a deeper understanding of a nation's politics, economics and lifestyle.

Cultural exchange, though, does not entail mutual understanding by two parties sharing identical or similar cultures. Instead, it consists of recognizing, and understanding, the unique and highly dissimilar points of each other's culture.

Only when such understanding exists can true cooperation and friendship evolve, thus leading to higher productivity that in turn enables global enrichment.

Dissimilarities in themselves do not prevent sympathetic understanding. If they did, then men and women would be incapable of loving each other. In the Orient, man and woman are interpreted in the context of Yin and Yang, a concept which is based on opposites coexisting in mutual harmony.

を、陽と陰として考えてきました。

▶日本文化のキーワード　さて、文化というつかみどころのないものを考えるために、日本の文化の特徴をとらえるキーワード、あるいはシンボルというものを一つ採り上げたいと思います。それは「雪月花」というものです。この「雪月花」を、別々ではなくて、三つ合わせて一つのコンセプトとして、われわれは考えております。これは一つの日本人の生き方を示すものでした。

　今回は、このひとつのシンボルイメージをキーワードにして、前半は日本の代表的な思想家や詩人たちの人生観、自然観を紹介し、後半は、建築や美術、その他の工芸品などを通して、日本人の文化を見ていきたいと思います。

「雪月花」と言いますと、日本人にとっても、ひじょうに古めかしく縁遠く感じるかもしれませんが、日本人の習慣や、歌舞伎のデザインなどを気をつけて見ると、この「雪月花」が至るところに見うけられます。また、旅館、料亭などで、たとえば着物の模様であるとか、飾られているインテリアのデザインなどに、きっと「雪月花」のデザインを発見することができるでしょう。

▶「お花見」「お月見」　今も生きている最もポピュラーな習慣には、春に桜を楽しむパーティである「お花見」と、「お月見」があります。私の子どもの頃は、月を見

▶ **A symbolic phrase** As a means of understanding the special nature of Japanese culture, which is intrinsically intangible, I would like to introduce you to a phrase which aptly symbolizes our culture. The phrase is *setsu-getsu-ka*, or "snow, moon and flowers."

In Japan this phrase is interpreted as one fundamental concept, rather than as an enumeration of three separate elements. Originally the phrase was used to express the Japanese way of life.

In this presentation, first I will explain the views of life and nature espoused by several of Japan's most renowned thinkers and poets. Later, using photo illustrations I will demonstrate how the concept came to be integrated in Japan's architecture, arts and crafts.

Although "snow, moon and flowers" may at first sound rather quaint and remotely removed from modern Japanese life, if we pause to look around us we can recognize its influence everywhere—in the Kabuki stage settings which you have seen, in the architecture of traditional inns, in kimono patterns, in modern interior designs. It is also supremely evident in Japanese customs.

▶ **Cherry blossom viewing party** Perhaps the foremost example of this kind is the "cherry blossom viewing party," which has become indelibly associated with the spring season.

When I was a child we also took part in "moon viewing parties" each autumn, and "snow viewing parties" continue to exist as part of the traditional tea ceremony.

What these various occasions do is to provide man with a means of uniting with nature at each season's turn, of verifying the bond of solidarity that exists between man and nature. In

ながらお団子を供えて食べたものです。「雪見」は今はあまりありませんが、やはり雪見のパーティが茶の湯に残っています。

　つまり、季節ごとに自然を愛し溶けこみ、そこで自然も含めた人間の連帯感、一体感を確認して、生きている喜びを味わうという心情が表わされています。また、日本の和歌や俳句、散文芸術では、四季のキーワードをよく用いています。

▶**古代と現在の共存**　こういうシンプルで古代的な感受性を、日本人は一面では引き継いでいます。これは世界でも珍しいことだと言えるでしょう。日本列島では、およそ2000年前から、このような文明が続いてきました。ご存じのように、現在の日本は島国ですが、古くは大陸と陸つづきだったと言われます。

　したがって、日本文化の底流には、ミクロネシア、ポリネシアからニューギニアにかけての南方海洋文化があると、指摘する人もいます。さらにその後は、インドで生まれた仏教文化であるとか、中国の道教・儒教文化などが流入しました。さらには、19世紀には西洋文明が爆発的に入って来ました。

　これらのさまざまな文化がほとんど奇跡的にうまく融合しています。

　そのためにわれわれ自身も、特に近年では、日本人であることを忘れるほどですが、一方では逆に、世界の中

this way, these occasions afford man the opportunity to reconfirm his joy in living.

It is at times such as these that we Japanese frequently are moved to poetry or other literary forms—forms in which "snow, moon and flowers" figure prominently.

▶**Ancient sensibilities**　There are few other countries in the world where simple sensibilities of such ancient origin can still be observed, even partially, in modern society. For over two thousand years, this unbroken thread of civilization has been present in the Japanese archipelago.

As you know, it is generally regarded that at one time the Japanese islands were an integral part of the Asian continent. Others theorize that the underlying source of Japanese culture is found in the South Sea cultures spanning from Micronesia and Polynesia as far as New Guinea.

Later, elements were added in the form of Buddhism, which is originally of Indian origin, and Taoism and Confucianism from China. Then starting in the 19th century, cultural influences also entered with explosive force from the West. Almost miraculously, all of these separate elements fused quite harmoniously in Japan.

The fusion has been so complete, in fact, that we Japanese, particularly today, tend to forget that we are Japanese. And yet at the same time we also tend to be universally regarded as a highly unusual, indeed inscrutable race. One reason lying behind this evaluation is the very fact that in Japanese culture so much of the old coexists and blends with the new.

でもひじょうに特殊で理解しにくい民族だと言われるようになってしまいました。その原因の一つには、こういう古代的なものと近代的なものが融け合って、併存しているという点にあります。

▶**初詣の群衆**　特殊な慣習の一つとして、たとえば、初詣があります。大みそかの真夜中の12時が過ぎ、新年に入ると同時に、一家そろって神社にお参りに行きます。

これはけっして信仰や戒律に強制されているわけではありませんが、その数は、日本全国で6000万人、7000万人ともいわれています。この数字は、動ける大人のほとんどが、神に詣でていることを示します。強制もされないのに、きわめて自然発生的に、けっして絶えることなく行なわれているところが実に不思議です。

私の米国の友人のある教授は「なぜ日本人というのは、元旦にみんなで神社に出かけるんだ。中国にも韓国にも、あんなことはまったくない。あの勢いで軍事的に、あるいは経済的に侵略されてはかなわない」と言って、不思議がっております。たしかに外国人には、日本の輸出貿易は、初詣の群衆のように映るのでしょう。

▶**地鎮祭**　また日本では、巨大で近代的なビルディングを建築する場合でも、さらには、それを世界的な建築家がデザインした場合でも、いざ、工事に取りかかろうと

▶ **The custom of *hatsumode*** Consider, for example, the custom of *hatsumode*, or visiting a Shinto shrine early after the start of a new year. Every year between 60 and 70 million Japanese, representing practically every able-bodied adult in the country, pay such a visit to a shrine during the first three days of the year.

Yet this practice is totally unrelated to any element of religious faith or doctrine. Instead it continues to be carried on from one generation to the next quite naturally.

An American friend of mine, a college professor, once asked me why we Japanese flock to shrines in such numbers at New Years, adding that there is no similar custom in China or Korea. He joked that after seeing the Japanese at hatsumode he could understand where Japan derived the human resources for its military and economic "invasions."

I then understood in quite vivid terms how Japanese export trade must appear in foreign eyes: just like the hordes that throng Shinto shrines at New Years.

▶ **Shinto ritual** As a second example, consider how we Japanese construct a new building. Even if the building is to be an ultramodern structure designed by one of the world's leading architects, before construction is started a simple bamboo framework is erected to serve as a temporary Shinto altar, a Shinto priest is called in, the ground is symbolically purified of any spiritual defilement, and prayers of appeasement are offered to the gods for benevolence and the safety of the construction workers.

This practice is followed at virtually all building sites even today, including, I would venture to say, the building we are gathered in right now, and for a fact I know that it was carried out at the construction site on the adjacent property. I too

いうときには、その敷地の四隅に竹を立てて、神を祭る簡単な祭壇を設けます。そして穢れをはらい、土地の神の心を鎮め、工事が安全に行なわれるよう祈願する行事が、いまでも、ほとんど必ず行なわれています。

　われわれが、今こうしているこのビルも、そうして建てられたはずですし、隣りにいま建ちつつあるビルでも同様です。この行事を「地鎮祭」といいますが、私も10年ほど前に家を建て替えたときには、やはり土地の神の心を鎮める祈りを捧げ、氏神神社の神官を招いて、お祓いをしました。

　それでは日本人が宗教的な国民かというと、必ずしもそうは言えません。よく使われる笑い話ですが、日本では、結婚式はだいたい神道で行ない、葬式は仏教で行なうのが普通です。

　これは欧米人の感覚で言えば、イスラム教で結婚式を挙げて、キリスト教でお葬式をするのと同じです。こうしたことを、日本人は、平然と行なっているということになります。

▶日本人の宗教的感情　では、日本人は、きわめて宗教的民族なのか、それとも宗教に無関心で無意識的なのか──これは、たいへんむずかしい問題です。

　ここに一つ、おもしろい統計があります。まず、日本人のうちで、なんらかの宗教行事、たとえば初詣とかお盆などを行なっていると答える人は、93％にのぼりま

made sure that the same procedures to appease the earth gods were duly taken when I rebuilt my own home about ten years ago.

This does not necessarily imply, however, that the Japanese are a religious people. Amusingly, Japanese weddings are normally conducted according to Shinto ceremony, based on traditional religious custom, while Japanese funerals are usually carried out according to Buddhist practices.

To the Western observer, this uninhibited mixing of religions seems as curious as would be the unlikely practice of blending an Islamic wedding, for instance, with a Christian burial.

●地鎮祭／*Jichinsai*

A Shinto ritual is performed prior to construction to ask for the earth gods' protection.

▶**The Japanese and their "religion"** Are the Japanese then an extremely religious race, or are they indifferent to and unconscious of religious inconsistencies? This is difficult to determine.

Interestingly, statistics show that as many as 93 percent of all Japanese take part in some form of religious custom,

す。では教義による信仰を持っているかといえば、イエスと答える人は十数％しかありません。どうやら、日本人は、組織的宗教に縛られるのは好まないようです。

　私は、やはり、ひじょうに古代的な宗教的感情というものが、日本人の深いところに根を下ろしているのではないかと思います。それを古神道(こしんとう)と呼ぶこともあります。では、その古い宗教的感情はどこから来るものでしょうか。それは、自然から、あるいは自然と人間との関係に求めることができます。

▶**日本人の自然観**　自然といいますと、とくに近代では、これを客観的に利用するものとして、あるいは自然科学の対象としてのみ捉(とら)えられていますが、日本では、古くから、自然をもっと深くて神秘的なものとして考えてきました。

　西欧でも、古代ギリシャでは、ネイチュアという言葉は、ある生み出す力を意味していました。それが中世になると、キリスト教によって、自然は神の下(もと)で人間と対立する被造物(ひぞうぶつ)と捉(とら)え直され、その考え方が、つい最近まで続いてきたわけです。

　したがって、ギリシャ・ローマでは、動いていく力、物を造り出す力そのものを、自然と呼んでいたわけです。日本人にとっての自然とは、この古代ギリシャのネイチュアという言葉に近いと理解すべきです。

　近代日本で最も傑出した有名な俳人・松尾芭蕉(まつおばしょう)

whether it be visiting a shrine at New Years, paying homage to ancestral graves at the time of *O-bon* during the summer, or whatever.

But when questioned whether they hold to a religious faith based on formalized doctrine, only slightly more than 10 percent answered in the affirmative.

Apparently the Japanese do not like to be bound by organized religions. I believe, however, that an extremely ancient religious sentiment lies deeply rooted in the Japanese—something that might be called "Old Shinto." Where does such an ancient religious sentiment come from? From nature, or from the relationship between nature and man.

▶**The Japanese concept of nature** Nowadays nature is typically viewed objectively as something which man can utilize to his own advantage, or as an object of scientific research. But in Japan, nature continues to have deeper, more mysterious significance.

In this respect Japan is somewhat similar to ancient Greece, where the concept of nature was imbued with a sense of creative power. This concept held sway until about the 12th century when it was reduced by Christianity and nature came to be seen as a creation of god poised in opposition to mankind.

In ancient Greco-Roman civilization the term for nature was applied directly to the idea of a creative act. The Japanese concept of nature should be understood in this same general sense.

Matsuo Basho (1644-94), Japan's most famous haiku poet,

（1644〜94年）は、自然を「造化」と呼んでいます。「造」はつくりだすこと、「化」は形を変えることです。この考え方は、古代ギリシャのネイチュアと見事に一致しています。つまり、ネイチュアは、ものではなく運動なのです。

　日本人の文化を考えるうえで、この自然という言葉が、ひじょうに重要です。「雪月花」は、そのシンボルです。つまり、雪は季節の移り変わり、時間の流れを表わし、月は宇宙・コスモス、空間の拡がりを表わします。花は時空にしたがって現われる存在現象の象徴といえます。

▶**自然は移り変わる**　この日本人の自然観の特徴を、三つの要素に分けて説明しましょう。

　第一に、先ほども述べたとおり、自然をけっして固定的なものと考えず、テンポラリー（一時的）なもの、四季のように移り変わるものとして捉える点です。

　つまり、植物が茂ったり、家畜が繁殖したり、人間が子孫を作ったりする力、こうした広く巨きな一種の性的なエネルギー、インドではこの宇宙的なエロスの力をシャクティと呼びますが、そのようなすべてを生み出す力と動きに満ちたものとして、自然を考えます。逆説的ですが、雪は新しい春の到来を予告しています。

▶**自然には秩序がある**　第二に、日本人は、自然は荒々

referred to nature as *zoka*, a word roughly translatable as "creation and transformation." This view coincides perfectly with the ancient Greek concept of nature.

The word "nature" is thus of extremely vital importance when considering the workings of Japanese culture, and snow, moon and flowers (*setsu-getsu-ka*) are its symbols.

Snow represents the changing of the seasons and the passage of time. The moon suggests the universe, the cosmos, the broad expanses of space. Flowers are a symbol of existence that appears in accordance with time and spatial references.

▶**Nature is temporary** Now let's discuss this view of nature based on its three fundamental elements.

First, as I mentioned earlier, nature is not constant or stationary but temporary and changing, like the never-ending cycle of the seasons.

Plants flourish, animals multiply and man procreates. This vast, cosmic, almost "sexual" energy—the Indians refer to it as *shakti*—is like a fluid movement filled with the power of creation. Paradoxically, snow acts as the harbinger of emerging spring.

▶**An element of harmony** Secondly, the Japanese believe that nature, in spite of its violence, always contains an element of harmony or order. It possesses a precious "something" that transcends humanity. In every natural landscape, in mountains and rivers, boulders and seas, in trees, there is a living god, a god founded on a premise of truth.

Sun worship is a manifestation of this belief, and the imperial line itself was for more than a millennium said to be

しく動いてはいるが、そこには必ずひとつの調和、秩序があると考えています。自然には、人間を超えたある崇(たっと)いものが含まれている、つまり自然の風景、山や川、巨岩や海、そして樹木など、そのそれぞれに神が宿り、その背景には真理があると信じています。

太陽崇拝はその代表的なもので、天皇は太陽神・天照大神(あまてらすおおみかみ)の直系の子孫と考えられていました。直感的にそう感じているのです。したがって、神の姿を描くかわりに、月や自然の風景を描いて、礼拝したりもしました。この場合、月は太陽を暗示します。

▶**自然との共存**　第三に、日本人は、自然を人間と対立したもの、あるいは人間が征服すべき対象としてではなく、その中でともに生きる、あるいは感情を交(か)わす、互いに愛情を持つ同じレベルのものとして考えています。つまり、自然も人間も、ともに仮の現象であり、輪廻転生(りんねてんしょう)してゆく運命を同じくするものと考えます。

梅の花は、雪の中にあって春の到来を告げ、宇宙を暗示し、花を眺めている人間の深い洞察(どうさつ)をシンボルしていると、禅僧の道元(どうげん)は言っています。

では、このような自然に対して、人間がどう生きているのでしょうか。当然のことですが、日本人は、自然と闘うよりも、自然に寄り添い、自然の法則に参加して生きてゆくという姿を採(と)ることになります。そのときの自我は、一度は自己否定され、時には自分を虚(むな)しくするこ

directly descended from Amaterasu, the sun goddess. This belief was intuitive, and for this reason the Japanese in worshiping would depict a natural landscape rather than a physical form of a god. The moon serves as a connotation of the sun.

▶ **Mutual emotional response** Thirdly, the Japanese do not view nature in opposition to mankind or as an object which man must conquer. Instead they believe that man lives harmoniously within nature, or that nature exists on the same level as mankind, a level marked by a mutual emotional response or love. In other words, nature and man are both but temporary phenomena destined to the cycle of transmigration.

Plum blossoms in the snow presage the coming of spring. According to the Zen monk Dogen (1200-53), this scene offers a deeper suggestion of the cosmos and the plum symbolizes the penetrating insight of the observer.

How then does man live in this natural context? As might be expected, instead of opposing nature the Japanese prefer to live in close communion with nature, obeying its rules. In doing so, they must engage initially in self-denial, at times extended to the point of emptiness.

This loss of one's self, however, does not equate with nothingness; rather, it is a void which is filled by nature. In Buddhism there is a concept known as *ku*, meaning "the void." It refers to the paradoxical state where a human being finds his true self in a higher dimension marked by a "satisfied void."

とになります。

とはいえ、自分をなくしたところは無(む)ではなく、むしろ自然によって充足された空虚(くう)です。仏教で空という言葉があります。ややパラドキシカルになりますが、充実した空虚と一致した、より高次元のほんとうの自己というものを、そこに感じるのです。

▶日本人にとっての労働とは何か　この自然に対する考え方を示す二つの例を挙げてみましょう。

ひところ、日本人はよく働きバチだとか働き中毒だと言われましたが、これは、労働という概念の文化的背景の相違からくる誤解です。よく言われることですが、西欧の概念では、労働とは一種のパニッシュメント――懲罰(ちょうばつ)です。楽園を追われたときから労働が始まった、というアダムとイヴのエピソードが、それを示しています。

しかし、日本では、古くから、働くということは農業生産でも鉱業でも焼き物を作る場合でも、自然が物を造化する力に、人間がコミットする、参加することにほかならない、という考えでした。

そのため自然が、組織や、あるいは近代的工場に置き換えられても、日本人は、その共同体の造り出す力にコミットすることに喜びを見出す、という形が生まれてくるわけです。

▶**"Worker bees"**   I would like to give two examples which illustrate this attitude toward nature.

The Japanese have for some time now been labeled "worker bees" or even "workaholics." This view, however, is a misconception based on cultural differences relating to the concept of labor.

As is frequently pointed out, in the West labor is considered a kind of punishment. This view traces back to the days of Adam and Eve when man became compelled to undertake labor after being chased from the Garden of Eden.

In Japan, by contrast, labor was from ancient times interpreted as a human commitment to join forces with nature in the creative process, whether it focused on agriculture, mining or pottery making.

In later days, when organizations or modern factories came to replace nature as the creative dynamo, this view of labor manifested itself as joy in committing oneself to the collective creative efforts of the group. Even in a daunting environment of heavy snow, there is joy to be found in labor.

▶**Interior space**   Several years ago the British criticized Japan for its cramped housing conditions in spite of the nation's vast achievements in GNP, referring to Japanese homes as "rabbit hutches." The Japanese, however, do not conceive of their homes as independent parcels of space cut off from nature.

The boundaries between interior and exterior are in fact extremely flexible, and in traditional homes a number of areas functioned somewhere in between, including verandas, hallways and the like. Man was content so long as he was a part of a spatial area that opened out toward nature.

A band of bunting hung beneath a cherry tree could instantly

▶空間の演出　もう一つの例として、日本はいくらGNPが増大しても、住居は狭く兎小屋のようだと英国人に揶揄されたことがありました。もっともな面もありますが、しかし、日本人は住まいの空間を、自然から四角に切り取って隔絶したものとして考えません。室内と室外の違いはきわめてフレキシブルで、縁側、廊下、土間、庇、軒などは、その中間ともいえる領域です。

　つまり、人は自然へ向かってひらかれた空間の一点になればいいのです。桜の木の下に幔幕を張れば、立派なパーティやセレモニーの室内ができます。ときに紅白の幕を張ると、それは祭りの空間になります。黒と白の幕を張ると、それは葬式とか不吉なことのスペースになります。緋の毛氈——赤い毛布を敷きますと、ひじょうに華やかなパーティの場所がそこに演出されます。

　日本人にとっての室とは、全自然に拡がってゆくひとつの手がかり、視点にすぎません。その中枢はどこにあるかといえば、部屋ごとに設けられたかつての祭壇、床の間にあります。貴族や大名たちの茶室が極端に狭いのはそのためです。自然と、より深く交渉するためです。そこには、月に象徴される真空観が見られます。日本では、破れた屋根から月を眺めるのは悲惨なことではなく、趣味的な生活とされているのです。

transform the outdoors to an "indoor" setting: red and white bunting for a festive occasion, black and white bunting for a funeral or solemn ceremony. Spreading out a bright red carpet of felt sets the stage for a party.

In this respect, a room is nothing but a springboard or stepping-stone from which man can enter the more expansive world of nature. Traditionally, the focus of each room was the Shinto ancestral altar or the special alcove known as the *tokonoma*.

The tea ceremony rooms of the aristocracy and *daimyo* feudal lords were also extremely small for this same reason, because they allowed their users to find deeper communion with nature. They also permitted them to view the moon, symbol of the great void. In Japan, viewing the moon through a rent roof was not a sign of destitution but at times a mark of knowing how to enjoy the finer things in life.

●野点 / Nodate
野外での茶の湯の会。
周囲を幔幕で囲い、
仮の空間を作り出す。

Outdoor tea ceremony. Bunting is set out to form a temporary barrier defining a spatial zone.

Ⅱ. 詩文学に表わされた日本人の心情

▶短い詩形・和歌と俳句　では、そのような日本人の考え方を、日本の歴史的な詩人・指導者のことばを通して、見てゆくことにします。そのよすがとして、まず、ノーベル賞を受けた日本の文学者・川端康成氏(かわばたやすなり)が、その受賞講演『美しい日本の私』の中で引用した和歌のいくつかを、私もここに紹介したいと思います。

　日本には、ひじょうに短い詩の形として、和歌、俳句というものがあることは、ご存じのことと思いますが、このような短い詩形は、いわゆる専門の文学者によって作られるばかりではありません。

　一般の生活者もまた、自分の愛や人生や思想を語るうえで、この短詩形をよく用いました。したがって現代でも、著名な政治家や経済人、ノーベル賞受賞の科学者なども、自分の心境を問われたときに、俳句、短歌を詠(よ)んで人々に示すということが行なわれています。

▶宇宙シンボルとしての風景　さて、最初の詩です。

　　春は花　夏ほととぎす　秋は月
　　　　冬雪さえて　すずしかりけり

　これは、道元(どうげん)禅師（1200〜1253年）という鎌倉時

II. The Japanese Heart As Expressed in Poetry

▶ **Haiku and *waka*** Now I would like to take a look at the Japanese attitude toward nature as it is reflected historically in the words of Japan's pre-modern poets and leaders. I will begin by introducing several poems which Yasunari Kawabata (1899-1972) cited in his acceptance speech upon receiving the Nobel Prize in Literature in 1968.

As you perhaps know, Japanese poetry has two prevailing forms, both extremely brief, known as haiku and *waka*. Traditionally these forms were widely espoused not only by professional writers but even by the everyday man as a means of conveying his love, thoughts or views on life. Even today everyone from famous politicians and economists to Nobel Prize-winning scientists, when asked their sentiments, will often avail themselves of the haiku or waka medium to speak their emotions through poetic metaphor.

▶ **An expression of Buddhist truth** Here then is the first poem, a 31-syllable (5-7-5-7-7) waka:

Haru wa hana	In spring, the flowers.
Natsu hototogisu	In summer, the cuckoo.
Aki wa tsuki	In autumn, the moon.
Fuyu yuki saete	In winter, the cold and
Suzushikarikeri	Crystalline snow.

The poem was written by Dogen, a Buddhist monk of the early Kamakura period who introduced Zen from China and set it on a solid footing in Japan. He wrote the poem as his

代の初期の人で、中国から日本に初めて禅宗を伝え、日本の禅を確立した僧の和歌です。彼が仏教の真理をうたったのがこの詩です。ところが、この詩はごらんのとおり、当たり前の自然の風景をうたっているだけです。

つまり、春は花が咲く、夏は木陰で鳥が鳴く、秋は月がひじょうに美しい、冬は雪が冷たく清らかだというわけです。いかにも幼稚な事実の羅列にすぎないように見えます。しかし、この誰にでもわかる当たり前のことを、当たり前として受け取るということ、そこに自然と人間が一体になった世界があるというのです。

これは、つまり雪月花の世界に通じます。特に、秋の夜の空にかかる月は、しばしば仏教の悟りの真理を表わすシンボルとして、たびたび用いられます。月が描かれているときは、つまり、そこに仏法の真理が象徴されていると解釈することができるのです。

▶聖フランチェスコと明恵上人　同じ鎌倉時代に生きたもう一人の高僧、明恵上人（1173〜1232年）という人は、次のような和歌を詠んでいます。この人はキリスト教世界におけるイタリアのアッシジの聖フランチェスコと並びくらべられる、ひじょうに純粋で清らかな生活を送ったことで知られています。

　　雲を出でて　われに伴う　冬の月
　　　　風や身にしむ　雪や冷たき

expression of Buddhist truth. As readily recognizable, it speaks of natural scenery, very conventional scenery, and no more.

"In spring the flowers bloom; in summer birds sing in the treetops; in autumn the moon is at its most beautiful; in winter the snow is cold and crystalline pure." Indeed, the whole thing may strike you as an altogether naive enumeration of accepted facts.

But it is this very ability to look upon the ordinary and recognize it as ordinary which is the world of "snow, moon and flowers" —a world where man and nature are at one.

The moon shining bright in the autumn sky is an especially frequent metaphor used in Buddhism, where it represents truth and enlightenment. A depiction of the moon is interpreted as a symbol of Buddhist truth.

▶ **The St. Francis of Japan** As an example, we have the following poem written by Myoe (1173-1232), another prominent Buddhist monk of the Kamakura period. Myoe is widely known for having lived an extremely pure and simple life, coming to symbolize for Buddhism the same ideals represented in Christianity by St. Francis of Assisi.

Kumo o idete	Winter moon,
Ware ni tomonau	Emerging from the clouds
Fuyu no tsuki	To keep me company.
Kaze ya mi ni shimu	What matters the piercing wind?
Yuki ya tsumetaki	What matters the icy snow?

There is a famous portrait of Myoe showing him deep in meditation cradled in the forked limbs of a large pine tree atop the mountain in northern Kyoto that is home to Kozanji Temple

明恵上人には、京都北部、高山寺(こうざんじ)近くの山中にあって、大きな松の木が二股に枝分かれしたところの上で、一人坐禅を組んでいる有名な肖像画があります（115ページ参照）。この僧は、月をひじょうに愛したことでも有名です。
　この歌に描かれているのは、彼が坐禅をしていると、月が後ろの山に出てくるという光景で、深い自然の山の中にあって、ほかにまったく人の気配はありません。
　さて坐禅を終わって自分の部屋に帰ろうとすると、いままで雲に隠れていた月がまた現われてきて、月は自分についてくるようだ。冬の風は身にしみるし、雪も冷たく感じるが、月はそれを明るく、当たり前のこととして照らしているというわけです。
　雲を出る月とは、迷いからさめた心境を指します。つまり、彼が深いメディテーション（瞑想(めいそう)）を通して、自然との温かいシンパシー（共感）を体験していたことがうたわれているのです。

▶**自然と一体になる心**　次の詩も、自然との温かい気持ちの交わりをうたっています。

　　山の端(は)に　われも入り　月も入れ
　　　夜な夜なごとに　また友とせん

(see page 115). In this work Myoe, who is well known for his love of the moon, is completely alone in his natural setting when the moon appears from behind a mountain ridge.

Later, when he finishes his meditation and is about to return to his room, the moon reappears, this time from behind a cover of clouds, whereupon he recites the just quoted poem. The moon, he says, seems to be following him. And though the winter winds may chill to the bone and the snow may be piercing cold, the moon shines its bright light on him as it always does.

This scene, the moon shining on the snow, represents Buddhist enlightenment: the mind awakening from illusion and uncertainty. From it we see how Myoe achieved a warm sympathy with nature through meditation.

▶**Man's relationship with nature** The following poem also speaks of the warm relationship between man and nature:

Yama no ha ni	I shall go behind
Ware mo iri	The mountain ridge.
Tsuki mo ire	Go there too, O moon.
Yonayona-goto ni	Night after night
Mata tomo to sen	We shall keep each other company.

As one meditates amid the solitude of nature, one's only companion is the moon. The moon and the meditator form a communion, eliciting a world of peaceful sympathy.

In the following poem Myoe took the concept one step further:

自然の中での孤独なメディテーションを行なうときに、友となるものはただ月だけである、月と自分とが相対して、そこに一つの静かな共感の世界が開かれている。
　さらにすすんで、

　　くまもなく　澄(す)める心の　輝けば
　　　　わが光とや　月思うかな

　ここで心というのは、自分個人の心を意味しているのではありません。自分の心が真理に達したとき、その光は月の光と同じである。自分が月を見ていると同時に、月が自分を見ている。すると、人間と月が入れかわり、自然と一体化して宇宙が一つのものと感じられる。そこにただ明るい月の光だけがある、というのがこの歌です。

▶**言葉なき詩**　彼はついに、月の光だけをうたった歌を詠(よ)むにいたります。それが次の詩です。

　　あかあかや　あかあかあかや　あかあかや
　　　　あかあかあかや　あかあかや月

　これはふざけた冗談のようにも聞こえますが、ここには、月を見物の対象としてのみ見ているのではなく、ひ

Kuma mo naku	My heart shines,
Sumeru kokoro no	Its pure brilliance
Kagayakeba	Knowing no bounds.
Waga hikari to ya	The moon will no doubt think
Tsuki omou kana	The light its own.

The "heart" spoken of here does not refer to the poet's own heart, i.e. his own mortal purity. What the poem says is this: "When the mind achieves enlightenment, man and nature become one. The heart glows and its light is the light of the moon. When one gazes on the moon, the moon gazes back. The moon and man change places, forming a greater cosmos, a cosmos filled only by the brilliant light of the moon."

▶ **"How bright the moon"**   Finally, Myoe brings his concept to its denouement in this unusual poem speaking of moonlight and nothing more:

Akaaka ya	How bright!
Akaaka aka ya	How bright, how very bright!
Akaaka ya	How bright!
Akaaka aka ya	How bright, how very bright!
Akaaka ya tsuki	How bright the moon.

Though these verses may sound comical, what they portray is not a visual enchantment with the brilliance of the moon but a state of oneness with the moonlight itself, the ultimate and purest state where man and nature are one. It is a poem that the Japanese love and highly respect.

Its protagonist has become so much a part of the moonlight that he is almost speechless. The lines of distinction between the viewer and that which is viewed melt away, and the

たすら月の光そのものになりきってしまった境地がうかがえます。これが自然と一致した純粋かつ最高の境地だとして、日本人はひじょうに好み、かつ尊敬します。月の光そのものになりきってしまって、言葉も出ない。見る者と見られるものとの対立が消えて、その関係そのものがクローズアップされている、そこに真実があるというのです。

▶松島で沈黙した芭蕉　同じように感動の極致、至高の体験を詠んだ俳句があります。江戸時代の、日本の最も偉大な詩人である松尾芭蕉が、松島という、美しい小島がたくさん浮かぶひじょうに美しい湾の風景をはじめて見たときに、詠んだ俳句です。

　　松島や　ああ松島や　松島や

　ただその土地の名前を繰り返すだけ。もはやいかなるレトリックも及ばない、どのような表現も表わすことのできない深い感動を、彼はこううたいました。ひじょうにシンプルで、幼稚にすら見えますが、日本人は風景に融け込み、自然と一致した最高の境地はここにあると評価しています。

▶桜の花の下で死を希った西行法師　このような境地を、かつての平安時代の宮廷の武人にして歌人、恋愛のため

inseparable relationship between the two becomes the focus of the poem. In this way, the poem thus speaks of the Buddhist truth.

▶ **The beauty of Matsushima** There is a famous haiku which describes a similar kind of emotional response to nature. Matsuo Basho, Japan's most famous poet of the Edo period, composed the following short poem upon seeing the beauty of Matsushima, a bay dappled with pine-graced outcrops, for the first time:

Matsushima ya	Oh, Matsushima!
Aa Matsushima ya	Ah, Matsushima!
Matsushima ya	Oh, Matsushima!

The poem is but a simple repetition of the name of the location and no more. Yet in it Basho acutely conveys the depth of his emotion, an emotion that cannot be conveyed through any amount of written description, an emotion transcending the efficacy of rhetoric.

Despite its seeming simplicity and naivete, the poem is a quintessential statement of how the Japanese can merge with their natural surroundings and reach a state of oneness with nature.

▶ **A poem prophesying one's death** This state of oneness has also been described by the poet-monk Saigyo (1118-90), a member of the Heian court who abandoned his life as an aristocrat warrior at the age of 20 to devote himself to Buddhism.

"When I compose a poem," Saigyo once said, "I am not writing a work of poetry. What I am doing is seeking the

20歳で世を捨て僧侶となった西行(さいぎょう)(1118〜90年)という人は、
「私は詩を詠んでも、実は詩を作っているのではない。では何をしているのか。実は自然の奥にある真実に出会うことを目指しているのだ」
と言っています。彼は、次のような美しい詩で、自分の死を予言しましたが、それも暗いものではありません。それどころか華やかで、あたかも自然への回帰をよろこび、永生(えいせい)を信じているかのようです。

　　願わくば　花のもとにて　春死なん
　　　　そのきさらぎの　望月(もちづき)のころ

そして、予言のとおり、釈迦涅槃(しゃかねはん)の記念日に合わせるように、彼はこの世を去りました。
このように、和歌も俳句も、日本人にとっては、単なる文語による表現芸術として留まるものではなく、人生のあり方への問いかけと答えそのものでした。

▶言葉は"ことだま"　有名な『源氏物語』という平安貴族の物語がありますが、そこでは、当時は和歌がうまいか下手かによって、男女の恋愛が成功するかどうかが決定された様子がうかがえます。また、政治的な地位さえも、詩の作り方の上手・下手によって決まったのが実情でした。

deepest truths of nature."

Saigyo also once wrote a poem prophesying his own death. It is a beautiful work not dark in tone but actually quite sanguine. It expresses the poet's joy at returning to nature, and seems to point to his belief in the everlasting.

Negawakuba	If wishes come true,
Hana no moto nite	Would that I might die
Haru shinan	In early spring
Sono kisaragi no	When flowers bloom
Mochizuki no koro	And the moon shines full.

Saigyo's wish was granted. He went to his eternal rest on the anniversary of Buddha's death, in early spring.

In this way, haiku and waka poetry were historically more than mere literary forms of expression to the Japanese. They embodied questions and answers concerning man's very own life on earth.

▶ **The autonomous power of language** In the well-known *The Tale of Genji*, a novel about the Heian court written in the 11th century, we learn that the romantic fortunes of a courtship were determined in this period by the degree of skill in waka composition demonstrated by the suitor and the suited. Even one's political fortunes, in fact, often depended on one's ability to turn a poetic phrase with grace.

Although it is rather pointless to pass judgment today on the wisdom of such criteria, it is worth noting that the Japanese long believed that language was more than simply a tool used to convey meaning. Language itself was imbued with an autonomous power of truth that transcended semantic nuances.

こういう時代がいいか悪いか、これは今、判断しても仕方ありません。しかし、日本人は言語もたんに意味を伝える道具ではなく、"ことだま（言霊）"といって、用途を越えたある真実の力を、言葉自体が独立してそなえていると信じていました。
　これまで紹介してきたような人々は、日本人にとって理想的な人物として、子どもの頃から学校教育を通じて教えられてきております。
　もちろん、そのような信条に生きることは容易ではなく、世俗的な生活者がほとんどです。しかし、このような理想的人物像は、誰しも認めているところです。
　したがって、「雪月花」というシンボルイメージで表わされる自然というものが、たんなる物質としての雪、月、花ではなく、その背景にある真実の世界を意味し、それに出会うことが、日本人の人生の目的であったということも分かるはずです。

▶良寛の生き方　中世とか古代とか、古い時代の話ばかりだとお考えかもしれませんが、150年ほど前、江戸時代においても、良寛（りょうかん）（1758〜1831年）という僧侶は、地位や名誉を得ることなく放浪し、ときに子どもと遊びつつ、その日その日を暮らしました。
　これは日本人の理想とする生き方の一つで、今も政治的、経済的に成功した上層階級の人間が、心の底に秘めている理想の姿は、何もせずに自然の中で自然と一致し

The poets I have cited here are all personages regularly included in standard educational curricula even today. To the Japanese they represent the highest ideals of Japanese culture.

This does not imply, of course, that it is easy to live according to these same principles nowadays, and to be sure there are very few who do. But they do represent widely accepted symbolic role models just the same.

From the foregoing discussion, we can now see that the phrase "setsu-getsu-ka"—snow, moon and flowers—is not merely an epithetic symbol of nature.

"Snow, moon and flowers" do not refer to snow, the moon and flowers as such, but rather to the world of truth that stands behind them. Coming to know this truth was the overriding goal of human life in Japan for centuries.

▶**Ryokan's way of life** Perhaps I have given you the impression that these matters were pertinent only in ancient times or the middle ages. But even as recently as about 150 years ago, during Japan's Edo period, there was a monk named Ryokan (1758-1831) who preferred to wander about the country playing with children rather than seek position or fame.

Ryokan's way of life also came to be viewed as an ideal in Japanese society, and even today there are many members of the upper echelons of society who have achieved political or economic success who secretly covet an ideal life in which they might be free to do nothing else but live amid nature and become one with nature.

Prior to his death Ryokan composed the following poem:

Katami tote	What shall I leave
Nani ka nokosan	As my legacy?

て暮らすという姿です。
　この良寛が、死に当たって次のような和歌をうたっています。

　　形見とて　何か残さん
　　　　春は花　山ほととぎす　秋はもみじ葉

　この歌は、先ほどの道元の和歌の影響の下に作られています。これもありふれた自然の風景、つまり春の花、山の鳥、秋のもみじを平凡にうたっていて、私が残す形見の品は何もないというだけの意味に思われますが、その背景には、やはり深い思想がかくされています。
　つまり自分が死んだ後も、自然はそのまま四季を繰り返している。その自然の中に、自分の生涯も死も抱きとられている。そのような絶対的真理としての自然の捉え方、それを、残る人々は私から学んでほしいと言っているのです。

▶**子どもと遊ぶ良寛**　厳しい世捨人の暮らしを送り、自分が死んでも、あとに残すものなどひとつもないとうたった良寛は、しかしながら、身の回りのささやかなものにも、楽しみを見出していました。とりわけ彼は、托鉢して歩きながら、子どもと出会うと一緒に遊ぶのが楽しみでした。
　その和歌を読みますと、

Haru wa hana	The flowers of spring,
Yama hototogisu	The cuckoo in the hills,
Aki wa momijiba	The crimson leaves of autumn.

The poem was influenced by the verse by Dogen I quoted several moments ago. In this case too, the poet offers a description which is quite commonplace: spring flowers, birds in the hills, autumn leaves.

On the surface it might seem that the poet is saying that he has no legacy to leave. Yet there is a far deeper significance lurking beneath the surface.

Namely, even after the poet dies the cycle of the four seasons will continue. And the poet recognizes his own life and death within this larger context, the context of nature, seen as an absolute truth. What the poet is doing is urging others to follow his example.

▶**Playing with children** This same Ryokan who lived a hard, ascetic life affording him no "earthly" legacy, did find pleasure of another kind in life. As he roamed the countryside as a mendicant priest seeking alms, he loved to stop and play with the children he would meet. The following poem describes his joy:

Kasumi tatsu	On this long spring day
Nagaki haruhi o	Misted with haze,
Kodomora to	I pass the day
Temari tsukitsutsu	Playing handball
Kono hi kurashitsutsu	With children.

One winter I went to visit the area where Ryokan spent his life, Echigo, along the Japan Sea coast, starting with his

霞(かすみ)立つ　永(なが)き春日(はるひ)を　子供らと
　　手鞠(てまり)つきつつ　この日暮らしつ

　私はある年の冬、良寛の故郷の出雲崎(いずもざき)から、彼が晩年を過ごした国上山(くがみやま)の五合庵(ごごうあん)を訪ねました。越後(えちご)は裏日本で、たいへん雪が深く、たいへん厳しい風土でした。驚いたことに土地の人々は、今でも「良寛さん、良寛さん」と、ひじょうに懐かしい思いをもって、150年以上昔の江戸時代の僧侶のことを語っていました。

　また、彼の書いた書は、今の日本の書道のなかで最高のもののひとつであり、高価に取引されています。たとえば一枚の掛軸が何千万円といった書があります。

▶**質素な暮らし**　次の和歌を読んでみましょう。

　　世の中に　まじらぬとには　　あらねども
　　　ひとり遊びぞ　我(われ)はまされる

　小さな庵(いおり)に住み、ひとつの鉢だけを手に、野原の草を摘(つ)み、子どもや農夫と語るというひじょうに質素な暮らしによって、今日でも、良寛は私たちに大きな影響を与え続けています。私たちは、子どものころから良寛のエピソードを聞いて育ったものです。

boyhood home of Izumozaki in Niigata Prefecture and going as far as Mt. Kugami, where he passed his later years in a hermitage called Gogoan. Echigo is a region of harsh, cold winters and heavy snowfalls.

Even today, more than a century after his death, the people of the area spoke of Ryokan with great warmth and familiarity.

His works of calligraphy, still regarded as one of the high points in the history of this art, fetch stupendous sums. A single hanging scroll, for example, might be traded at upwards of 20 or 30 million yen.

▶**The simple life**　　Here then is another poem by Ryokan.

Yo no naka ni	It is not so
Majiranu to ni wa	That I seek
Aranedomo	To shun the world;
Hitori-asobi zo	I am just better
Ware wa masareru	At playing alone.

The simple life led by Ryokan—sleeping in a humble hermitage, a begging bowl his only possession, plucking the grasses in the plain, talking with children and farmers—continues to have a great influence on our lives as Japanese even today.

▶**Falling in everlasting love**　　As children we grew up hearing stories about him, stories like how he remained so pure in heart that at the age of 69 he fell in love with a nun only 29. As good luck would have it, the affair was to result in everlasting love. The following is a poem which Ryokan composed at this time:

▶**永遠の女性との出逢い**　彼はひじょうに純粋な気持ちを持っていたので、69歳の時に29歳の尼さんと恋をします。幸運なことですが、彼ははじめて永遠の女性に巡り合ったのです。

そのときの歌がこれです。

　　いついつと　待ちにし人は　来(きた)りけり
　　　今は相見(あいみ)て　何か思わん

ひじょうに率直に、待ちこがれた恋人との出逢いのよろこびがうたわれています。

以前、このような良寛の話を外国の方(かた)にお話したところ、現代の日本の経済人も、本当にそういうことを考えているのかという質問を受けました。これは、はなはだ個人的なことで、答えるのはむずかしいことですが、たとえ、実行はできなくても、心の底に、理想として、そのようなイメージを持っているということは言えます。

事実、私の高等学校の先輩で、日本の代表的銀行の頭取(とうどり)をしているK氏は、良寛の心酔者です。

▶**茶の湯と書道**　明治の日本資本主義形成のとき、三井財閥を築いた益田鈍翁(ますだどんおう)は、大茶人でした。今日でも、成功した経済人のなかに、茶を楽しむ人は数多くいます。茶の湯は、このごろますます盛んになっています。伝統的な茶の湯が、上流階級の男性の社交的なパーティとし

Itsuitsu to	The one I have long
Machinishi hito wa	Waited for
Kitarikeri	Has come, at last.
Ima wa aimite	Gazing at each other now,
Nani ka omowan	What more could I wish for?

It is a very frank poem speaking of the poet's joy at meeting his long-awaited love.

During a similar talk which I gave to foreign visitors last year, someone asked me if Japan's modern-day, economics-oriented leaders continue to think in the same vein as Ryokan.

Though this is a very difficult question to answer, since it bears so heavily on each individual, I believe that somewhere deep in their hearts they do carry this same kind of image as an ideal, even if they are unable perhaps to achieve it.

For example, I know a man, one of my seniors from high school days, who now presides as president of one of Japan's largest banks, who is a great devotee of Ryokan.

▶**The tea ceremony and calligraphy**   Mr. Don'o Masuda, the man who was instrumental in building up the great Mitsui Zaibatsu, or financial combine, when capitalism gained a foothold in Japan during the Meiji period, was known as an avid enthusiast of the tea ceremony. And today there are many economically successful individuals like him who enjoy performing traditional tea ritual.

In fact, the tea ceremony is enjoying a great wave of popularity nowadays. What is surprising is that this discipline, which was traditionally viewed as a social amenity of the male members of upperclass society, is now serving precisely the

て、中世と同じように、今、再び盛んになっているのは驚くべきことです。

また、字を書くこと、いわゆる書道も、男女を問わず、生活を豊かにする芸事(げいごと)として、最近、たいへん盛んになっています。これらを見ますと、経済的豊かさは、むしろ日本人に、伝統的な生活を復活させつつあるという気がします。

▶"大和心(やまとごころ)"　こうして見ると、日本人は四季の中で花や月と暮らしていたということになり、外国の方は、これを現実ばなれした誇張だと考えるかもしれません。もちろん、近代日本人の生活様式は変わりましたが、どのような気持ちで暮らしているかという点では、案外、古代から変わらない心情が流れているといえます。

19世紀の中ごろの革命家であり、初めてアメリカとの国交を開こうとした進歩的な思想家・吉田松陰(よしだしょういん)(1830〜59年)ですら、こういう歌をうたっています。

　　身はたとい　武蔵(むさし)の野(の)べに　くちぬとも
　　　　とどめおかまし　大和魂(やまとだましい)

まさに、自然への回帰をうたっているのです。

▶芭蕉による結論　先ほど紹介した松尾芭蕉は、有名な

same social function today as it did during the middle ages.

Calligraphy too is recently quite popular, among men and women alike, as a cultural pursuit which enriches one's life. In this way, I believe that Japan's modern economic affluence is actually causing a rebirth of interest in traditional Japanese lifestyles.

▶**The Yamato Spirit**　From my description so far, we must conclude that the Japanese pass their lives in close communion with flowers, the moon and the changing seasons.

Perhaps this strikes you, the non-Japanese, as an exaggeration, and without question Japanese lifestyles have changed in modern times. Still, to a surprising degree, the fundamental Japanese attitude toward life seems to remain unchanged from ancient times.

Even Yoshida Shoin (1830-59), a progressive thinker and revolutionary of the mid-19th century who made the first attempt to establish diplomatic relations between Japan and the U.S., left the following poem to posterity:

Mi wa tatoi	Even should my body
Musashi no nobe ni	Decay beneath Musashi Plain,
Kuchinu tomo	Forever will I keep
Todomeokamashi	The Yamato Spirit,
Yamatodamashii	The spirit of Japan.

The poem clearly speaks of a return to nature.

▶**"A frog jumps in —"**　Matsuo Basho, the renowned haiku poet mentioned earlier, is best known for the following verse:

Furuike ya	The old pond.

古池や　蛙(かわず)飛び込む　水の音

　という俳句で知られていますが、彼は日本人の生き方を次のように語っています。
「風雅におけるもの、造化(ぞうか)にしたがいて四時(しいじ)を友とす。見るところ花にあらずということなし。思うところ月にあらずということなし」
　この言葉は、先ほど申した「雪月花」と同じ考え方を端的に示しています。すなわち人間と自然との共感と共生をあげ、そのことによって、より大きな自然と一体化して充実感を味わうことができる、という考え方です。
　日本人の会社への忠誠心や、共同体への帰属意識が異常だとよく指摘されますが、これは必ずしも人間関係によるものではなく、その根底には、自然と人間の関係に対する伝統的な姿勢があるわけです。

▶雪月花と一体化　このように申しますと、個人がなくなり、自己を否定するように聞こえるかもしれませんが、そうではありません。自分より大きなシンパシー、あるいはムーブメントにエンゲージすることによって、超越的真理に一体化するということは、日本の古神道や仏教の教えるところです。
　つまり美しい自然のなかにいるとき、人は、最も親しい友情を思い出す、ということを中国の白楽天(はくらくてん)という詩人が詩に書いています。

Kawazu tobikomu	A frog jumps in —
Mizu no oto	The sound of water.

Basho is said to have described the Japanese philosophy toward life with these words: "The man of refinement lives in harmony with the four seasons, according to the principles of nature. He views only flowers; he ponders only the moon."

These guiding principles point to the same elements of nature which I discussed before, namely, snow, the moon and flowers. What Basho is saying is exhorting his fellow man to respond to and live in harmony with the workings of nature, thereby to reach a state of inner fulfillment where he becomes one with nature.

It is often pointed out that the Japanese demonstrate an "abnormal" degree of loyalty to their company or extreme group consciousness. I believe that, fundamentally, these phenomena are not necessarily outgrowths of interpersonal relationships, but rather of a traditional attitude toward the relationship between man and nature.

▶ **Reaching oneness with nature** A statement such as this may seem to negate or deny the significance of the individual, but this is not so. According to ancient Shinto and Buddhist precepts, it is through his engagement in a greater sympathy or greater movement that the individual human being is able to become one with the transcending truth.

For example, it is when he is surrounded by the beauties of nature that man remembers his most intimate friendships. This idea was aptly described by the famed Chinese poet Bo Juyi (772-846):

Companions in music, poetry and wine

琴詩酒の友は　みなわれをなげうち
　　　雪月花の時　最も君を憶う

　音楽やパーティのときの友だちは、縁がなくなれば私を離れていく。しかし雪月花と一体化しているとき、同じ心境の分かる者たちは、しみじみと友情を味わうことができる。つまり自然によって支えられた人間のコミュニティというものが、ここでは深く強く歌われています。

▶「座」の文学　こうして人間同士も、自然を基礎にして、何よりも協調を大切にします。これは近代産業の労働関係ばかりではなく、先ほど紹介した俳諧をつくる場合でも同じです。というのは、数人、ときに十数人が一間に集まって、俳諧を作るという文学形態があるのです。日本では、これを「座」と言います。グループとかサークルに近いものですが、詩とか文学というような、個人の気持ちを表現する場合ですら、多人数が集まるというのはたいへん驚くべきことと言えます。
　つまり、一人が一行の詩を書くと、次の人がその次の行を書く、同席する人々が次々と一行ずつ書き加えていく、その結果、一つの詩が出来上がる、つまり合作になるわけです。こういうことは、ほかの文化では考えられません。一種のシリーズポエムというものです。

> All cast me aside.
> It is when gazing
> At the snow, moon and flowers
> That I think of you most.

Friends who gather to enjoy music or festive occasions, the poet says, may one day grow distant from each other. But those who have shared the experience of reaching oneness with nature (sun, moon and flowers) know the true meaning of friendship.

With this poem, the poet proclaims his strong belief that a truly sympathetic human community exists only through the fundamental support of nature.

▶**Linked verse** From this we see that, starting from the context of nature, human beings must attach highest priority to a commitment of mutual cooperation. This is true not only in modern-day labor relations in industry, but was also the case in certain ancient forms of poetry composition.

Consider the Japanese poetic form known as "linked verse." Several persons, sometimes as many as ten or more, would gather together in one room to engage in collective composition. Normally poetry, or literature in general, is considered an expression which is individualistic in orientation. But in the case of Japanese linked verse, composition was a joint effort of five or ten or even more participants.

One poet would begin by writing the first verse; this would be continued by a second poet who would add a second verse; and so on by each participant until an entire poem was completed. Collective literary composition such as this— "serial poems," if you will—must seem very surprising, surely, and it is an idea inconceivable in other cultures.

▶共同作業の喜び　先ほども紹介した芭蕉は、この「座」について驚くべき発言をしています。彼はいつも、命がけで短詩形の言葉を磨(みが)きましたが、その彼が、「作品を作り上げることが目的ではない」と言うのです。「一緒に座をつくり、一つの創作活動に参加する、そこで喜びを味わうことが大事だ、出来上がった作品は、そのまま捨ててもいい」とまで言っています。つまり、詩を作る場合においてすら、共同作業をする喜びのほうが、その結果よりも大事だというわけです。

　ここで重要なことは、これが詩とか俳諧という特殊な場合に限るものではなく、ひろく日本人の生活の基本的なシステムになっているということです。もちろん、近代的な生活のなかでは、こうしたことは一見忘れられ、毎日少なくなっているように見えますが、たとえばエンターテイメントの場や、民謡の席などで、このような気持ちがよく現われているのを見出すことができます。

　さて、いくぶん話が抽象的になりましたので、ひとつ図版を通して、日本の歴史的な文化遺産の数々を紹介し、そこにどのように日本人の意識が現われているかを、説明していくことにしましょう。

▶ **The pleasure in joint effort** Basho once made a rather surprising statement about these joint compositions. Though he is known for the great pains he took to polish each turn of phrase, he himself stated that poetic composition was not his intrinsic objective. More important, he said, was the joy to be gained from partaking in a collective creative effort. In fact, he added, it wouldn't matter at all even if the finished work were discarded.

In other words, more significant than the actual result was the pleasure acquired in jointly striving toward the end, even in the case of poetry.

What is important to recognize here is that this concept expounded by Basho was not limited to poetry alone, which in itself is something out of the ordinary, but extended to all aspects of Japanese life.

In modern society, of course, such a concept may seem forgotten or gradually diminishing. Yet it can still be readily detected in many areas such as popular entertainment, traditional folk songs and the like.

Well, I see that I have become somewhat abstract in my discussion. Now I would like to introduce some photo illustrations. Together let's examine in what ways they reflect the special character of the Japanese.

Ⅲ. 図版で見る日本人の心と形

1. 日本の歴史を概観

▶**日本民族の起源**　はじめに、大雑把(おおざっぱ)に日本の歴史を見ておきましょう。現在、日本は島国ですが、歴史をさかのぼりますと、ほぼ1万年から2万年以前には、アジア大陸とつながっていたと言われています。それは考古学的に、マンモスの化石が発見されていることからも明らかです。

　最近、考古学の研究が進むにつれて、日本民族の起源は、ますます古く20万年前ぐらいまでさかのぼることがわかってきました。そして、それには大きく分けて、二つの流れがあると考えられています。

　一つの流れは、南方、たとえば東南アジア、ミクロネシア、ポリネシア、ニューギニアなどから移住してきた農耕民族の流れ。一方は、北方のユーラシア大陸のモンゴルなどから、中国や、朝鮮半島を通って南下してきた騎馬民族の流れです。

▶**縄文(じょうもん)文化と弥生(やよい)文化**　したがって、日本の文化には、北方の騎馬民族的なものと、南方の農耕民族的なものの二つの要素が、からみ合っていると言われています。考古学的には縄文(じょうもん)文化、また弥生(やよい)文化という言い方で、この二つの流れを特徴づけています。

III. Japanese Mind and Form

1. Overview of Japanese History
▶ **Origins of the Japanese race**　In this section, I would like to begin with a general introduction to Japanese history. Although Japan today is a nation of islands, it is said that 10,000 to 20,000 years ago these outcrops were still an integral part of the Asian mainland. This theory is supported archaeologically by the discovery in Japan of mammoth fossils (*Mammuthus primigenius*).

With recent progress in archaeological research, we now know that the Japanese race dates back even further than previously thought, to about the 10th century B.C. Broadly speaking, these origins follow two streams.

The first traces to the north and consisted of horse-riding tribes from Mongolia and elsewhere in the Eurasian continent who eventually arrived in what is now Japan via China and the Korean peninsula. The second is a migration of agrarian tribes from the south, including areas such as Southeast Asia, Micronesia, Polynesia and New Guinea.

▶ **The Jomon and Yayoi cultures**　Japanese culture, in consequence, is said to have originated through the intertwining of these two separate elements: the equestrian group of the north and the agricultural group of the south.

Archaeologically these two strains of early Japanese culture are differentiated as the Jomon and Yayoi cultures, respectively. In reflection of its northern origins, the Jomon culture was dynamic and active. The Yayoi culture, based on the southern agrarian tribes, was more peaceful and passive. These

この騎馬民族的なものである縄文文化は、ダイナミックでエネルギッシュな性格を持っています。弥生文化は農耕民族的で、静かでシンプルな要素を持っています。それらが綯い合わされて、その後の日本文化のさまざまな場面に姿を表わします。
　日本人が外国の方からしばしば誤解を受ける理由の一つは、ここにあると、私は考えます。

▶**日本史の時代区分**　考古学的な時代につづいて、歴史時代に入りますと、およそ紀元後500年ぐらいに国家が成立します。古代は飛鳥、奈良、平安時代と、首都の場所によって、さらに三つに分けられます。
　その後、西暦1192年に鎌倉幕府が成立し、中世に入ります。江戸に幕府が移るのが17世紀で、19世紀、開国から明治維新を経て近代に入る、これが最も大きな三つの分け方です。古代は天皇と貴族の時代、中世は将軍の幕府と武家の時代、そして近代は庶民の時代です。

▶**仏教伝来と伝統文化**　もう少し詳しく分けて見ますと、歴史的古代になってからの大きな事件は、6世紀に仏教が日本に入ってきたことです（538年）。以来、飛鳥・奈良を中心に、アジア仏教文化が花を開きます。さらに奈良に都が定められたとき（710年）、はじめて中国の官僚制度が移入されました。
　都が今の京都に移り平安時代が始まると、貴族社会が

contrasting traits later manifested themselves in Japanese culture in various ways at various times, and even today the Japanese are often misunderstood abroad as a result, I believe, of their racial complexities.

▶**Subdivisions of Japanese history** Following these archaeological origins, the historical era in Japan traces to about A.D. 500 and the establishment of a nation-state.

The subsequent history of Japan then falls broadly into three phases. The "ancient period" spans the Asuka, Nara and Heian periods, each named for the site of its capital city in the area corresponding to modern-day Kyoto and its environs.

The "middle ages" then began in 1192 when the Shogunate government was set up far off to the east in Kamakura, and continued on through the period after the Shogunate was relocated to Edo, which is now Tokyo, in the 17th century. The "modern era" dates to the Meiji Restoration of the 1860s, just after the archipelago was finally opened to the outside world.

Viewed from a different angle, the ancient period was a time of emperors and aristocracy; the middle ages were a period of Shoguns and samurai; the modern era is Japan as we generally know it today.

▶**The introduction of Buddhism** Upon closer examination, several events of major importance stand out in the historical era. In the ancient period, topping the list was the introduction of Buddhism from the Asian continent in the 6th century (538) and its subsequent flourishing in the Asuka and Nara periods. Another significant development was the adoption of a Chinese-style bureaucratic system after the capital was moved to Nara in 710.

Later, after the capital was again relocated to what is now

8 縄文式土器
Jomon pottery

9 色絵藤花文茶壺　野々村仁清作　17世紀
Tea Jar with Wisteria Design, by Nonomura Ninsei, 17th c.

作られ、宮廷文化が成熟します。貴族にかわって武士が権力を握るのは、鎌倉時代からです。いわゆる封建時代となり、日本の伝統文化が確立します。領地と城を持ついくつかの大名が互いに激しく争った末、徳川将軍によって政治的に統一され、江戸幕府が開かれます。それが17世紀の初め（1603年）です。

▶鎖国（さこく）　この江戸時代の始まる少し前から初めにかけて、ポルトガルやスペインから渡来したキリスト教宣教師が活躍して、一時期、海外文化との交流が盛んに行なわれたのですが、江戸時代になって30余年経過したとき（1639年）、鎖国が断行され、海外貿易を表面的には禁止することになったことはご存じのとおりです。

　この鎖国は、1853年、アメリカのペリー提督（ていとく）が日本に来て国際交流の門を開くまで続きました。そして、アジアでは奇跡的といわれる近代社会革命を行ない、明治維新を迎えました。以来、すでに1世紀を越えています。

▶鎖国の歴史的評価　この鎖国と維新とが、近代日本の性格を決定するうえで大きな影響があったとは、よく指摘されることです。鎖国がプラスであったか、マイナスであったか、議論が分かれています。マイナスとする考え方は、言うまでもなく世界の進歩に遅れたという考えです。

Kyoto at the start of the Heian period, an aristocratic society emerged and court culture reached a high level of sophistication.

During the middle ages, the aristocracy was then supplanted by a warrior class during the ensuing Kamakura period. Japanese "traditional" culture took firm root during the feudal period which came thereafter and which was marked by incessant in-fighting among rival *daimyo*, or warlords, who possessed their own fiefs and castles.

Eventually, this warfare produced one triumphant leader, the Tokugawa Shogun, who succeeded in uniting the nation into a single political entity, the "Edo Shogunate," in 1603, marking the start of the Edo period.

▶**The closing of Japan**   The early Edo period, and the years leading up to it, was a time of much activity in Japan by Portuguese and Spanish missionaries preaching faith in Christianity. For a time these exchanges with foreign culture flourished on a grand scale, until 1639 when the Shogunate determined to close the country to all outside influences, including, at least on the surface, all trade relations.

This closed-door policy continued for over two centuries until America's Commodore Matthew Perry reopened the door to international exchanges in 1853. Just over a decade later, Japan went through the upheaval of the Meiji Restoration, a modern social reform nothing short of miraculous for an Asian country at that time.

▶**Effects of national seclusion**   As is often indicated, the closing of Japan for two hundred years and its subsequent reopening through the Meiji Restoration were instrumental in forming the character of the nation as it entered the modern

10 伊勢神宮　内宮正殿

Main sanctuary of Ise Shrine

11 出雲大社　本殿

Main sanctuary of Izumo Shrine

逆にプラスもあったと積極的に評価する考え方は、鎖国によって文化の成熟を促し、官僚制度が完備されたということです。日本の近代化に際して西洋の制度・文化が流入してきたときに、破滅的な混乱を受けないで消化することができたのも、成熟した文化と制度によるものであって、これは江戸時代300年間に発達し、整備された官僚制度のおかげだという歴史家もいます。

　たとえば、今日の貿易摩擦と同じようなエピソードが残っています。軍艦で浦賀に入ったアメリカの使節は、日本との通商・外交を開くことを求めますが、その出先機関の官僚の手続がたいへん複雑で、米国の使節は交渉を進めることができません。その結果、日本政府は多くの時間を稼ぎ、いまだかつてない新しい事態に対応することができました。

　このような官僚的テクニックは、すでに江戸時代に成立していたというのです。

　アジアにおける日本の近代化は、きわめて劇的、かつ奇跡的だとさえ言われておりますが、それに先立つ200年余の鎖国によって成熟した江戸時代の文化、教育の普及と、よく組織された官僚制度を忘れることはできません。

period.

Opinions vary as to whether the prolonged closure of Japan was, in the long run, a negative or positive influence. Those who see it as a negative influence cite, of course, the resulting backwardness of the nation compared with the progress seen in the rest of the world.

On the other hand, those who view this period of isolation as a positive influence point to the opportunity that gave the native culture time to mature and the bureaucratic system time to perfect itself. These same historians support their view with the contention that it was this maturity of Japanese culture and the bureaucratic system, developed during the three centuries of the Edo period, that enabled Japan to assimilate Western systems and culture without any destructive turmoil during the ensuing period of modernization.

As an example, there is an historic episode from those days that greatly resembles the problem surrounding trade friction today. When American warships landed at Uraga, in what is now Kanagawa Prefecture, and requested the opening of trade and diplomatic relations with Japan, bureaucratic procedures at the local government outpost were so complicated that the American envoy was unable to make any progress in the negotiations.

As a result, the Japanese government succeeded in stalling the Americans for quite some time—no small feat considering its complete inexperience in diplomatic matters of this sort. Exploitation of bureaucratic red tape to one's own advantage was thus a technique that was already firmly established in Japan back in the Edo period.

It is often said that the modernization of Japan was extremely dramatic and indeed miraculous given the conditions of Asia at that time. In analyzing Japan's success, however, one must

12　法隆寺　五重塔と金堂　7世紀

Five-storied pagoda and Kondo Hall (left), Horyuji Temple, 7th c.

13 金堂壁画　観音菩薩　7世紀

Kannon Bodhisattva, wall painting, Kondo Hall, 7th c.

▶**天皇について**　一般に、日本のこのような体制的制度、政治・経済的なシステムは、8世紀以来、かなり整備され運営されていたということができます。というのは、天皇は宗教的なシンボルとして、政治・経済から切り離されていたからです。祭司権と政治・経済の権力は、分離して機能し、西欧や他のアジアの国のような絶対的独裁者は、かつて日本に存在したことはありません。

つまり、政治・経済・技術は、権力の表現ではなく、機能として能率的に整えられていました。政治と宗教を、また経済と人間的生活とを分離することによって、伝統の維持と、外国からの新しい思想や技術に対する対応が、破滅的なトラブルを起こさないで解決されたと言うことができます。これを当時の人々は〈和魂洋才〉と言いました。伝統的な生活信条を本質的に保ちながら、近代文明を「機能」イコール「才」として、採り入れるのです。

天皇制の問題は、不幸な第二次世界大戦にかかわって、今日では政治的にみることは、ひじょうにデリケートな問題ですが、少なくとも歴史的には、むしろ有効に働いてきたと言うことができます。

このような文化と制度の二面性、また文化の中の激しいものと穏やかなものとの二面性が、伝統的文化の中にも流れています。では、これからそれを、建築や美術、造形の中に見ていくことにしましょう。

keep in mind the highly mature state of Edo culture, widespread education and a well-organized bureaucracy that resulted from more than two hundred years of isolation from outside influences.

▶ **The Japanese imperial system**　In general it may be said that Japan's organized political and economic systems were already well established and in operation by the 8th century.

This was possible because the Emperor was viewed as a religious symbol separate from the political and economic systems. Religious authority and politico-economic power were exercised independently, and at no time did Japan give birth to absolute monarchs as seen in other Asian nations or the West. Political and economic skills were not accepted as expressions of authority, but were effectively controlled as functions.

This separation of politics and religion, or economics and everyday life, it might be added, enabled Japan, during the Meiji period, to maintain its traditions and respond to the new ideas and technologies of outside nations without destructive consequences.

At the time, this fundamental separation of values was defined by the catchword *wakon-yosai*, meaning "Japanese spirit, Western learning." The phrase was widely used to exhort adoption of the technical advantages of modern civilization while still maintaining a basic adherence to traditional Japanese lifestyles and beliefs.

Although today the Japanese imperial system is an extremely delicate political issue due to its unfortunate role in World War II, it is safe to say that, at least in its historical context, it was a system that worked quite effectively.

The dichotomy between culture and system, and the

14 中宮寺　菩薩半跏像　7世紀

Bodhisattva, Chuguji Temple, 7th c.

15 薬師寺　聖(しょう)観音像　8世紀

Sho Kannon Bodhisattva, Yakushiji Temple, 8th c.

2. 古代の世界（飛鳥・奈良・平安時代）

▶**神道の神殿**　まず、**図版⑩**は7世紀末に建てられた伊勢神宮です。古代日本人の住居をモデルとしています。これは神殿で、日本の天皇の祖先であり、太陽神である天照大神(あまてらすおおみかみ)をまつっています。この神は、同時に神道の神々のなかでの最高神とされています。

穢(けが)れのない五十鈴川(いすずがわ)の流れを前にし、深い杉林に囲まれて、清らかな玉砂利(たまじゃり)が周囲に敷かれています。

ごらんのように、特徴的な点は、いっさい人工的な装飾を用いないで、白木(しらき)をそのまま用いていることです。当時は、すでに仏教が伝来していますから、装飾的な仏教建築が次々と造られていましたが、日本人は自分たちの伝統的な神を祭るのに、古代からのシンプルな住居の形式によって神殿を建てたわけです。

▶**式年遷宮(しきねんせんぐう)**　また、今残っている伊勢神宮は、1200年の形をそのまま伝えていると言えます。どうして、木造でそういうことが可能であるかと申しますと、実は、日本語で〈式年遷宮(しきねんせんぐう)〉と言いますが、神殿を20年ごとに造り替えているからです。ここには伝統の維持ということで、きわめて日本的な考え方が現われています。

つまり、20年ごとに伊勢神宮は古くなっても新しいままでも、壊れても壊れなくても、定期的に建て替えます。右の敷地にあるものを壊して、左に建て替えてしまうわけです。ですから建物そのものは異なっても、原型

dichotomy between aggressive and passive tendencies simultaneously present within Japanese culture, persisted through the entire flow of traditional culture. Now let's see how these dualities were manifested in Japanese architecture and the arts.

2. The Ancient Period (Asuka, Nara, Heian)

▶**Ise Shrine**　Figure **10** shows the Ise Shrine, probably the nation's most important Shinto monument, which dates to the late 7th century. It is patterned after Japan's ancient domestic dwellings. Here we see the main sanctuary where the Sun Goddess Amaterasu, mythical ancestor of the imperial family and supreme deity in the Shinto pantheon, is enshrined. The shrine is situated along the bank of the pristine Isuzu River, deep in a forest of cedars, surrounded by a clean carpet of pebbles.

As you see, the shrine is unusual in that it is built of unpainted wood completely free of all artificial decoration. Although more decorative buildings were, of course, already in existence at the time, modeled after Buddhist architectural styles, the contemporary Japanese obviously felt that a simple design patterned on native dwellings of ancient origin was more appropriate for a structure enshrining their own traditional gods.

▶**Preservation of tradition**　The Ise Shrine which stands today retains the exact design first devised 1,200 years ago. How could such a feat be possible with a wooden structure? The secret lies in the fact that the shrine is razed and rebuilt every twenty years. This practice, unique to the Japanese, is regularly carried out in order to preserve tradition.

Every twenty years, whether it is in need of repair or not,

16 薬師寺　東塔(とうとう)　8世紀

Three-storied pagoda, Yakushiji Temple, 8th c.

17　三仏寺　投入堂　11世紀

Nageiredo, Sanbutsuji Temple, 11th c.

は正確に維持されます。同じパターンをすぐ隣りで踏襲していくからです。

　パルテノン、ローマの神殿、ゴシックの教会などは石で造られ、その建物自体が年月を超えて永久に持続しています。しかし、日本人は初めから神殿をひじょうに壊しやすく造り、テンポラリーに壊して同じものを建て替えるという方法を採りました。つまり、実体は違うけれども、モデルとシステムを保存し、その物自体は変わっても、同じ神殿が永遠に続くという方法を選んだことになります。

　このような考え方は、先端科学技術にも、きわめて暗示を与えるものだと思われます。ここには、コンピュータシステムに似た感覚があります。つまり、物質それ自体よりも、情報のネットワークのほうが現実的だということです。

　また、この白木の建物は、見ておわかりのとおり、きわめて機能的です。特別な装飾は何もなく、屋根を支える柱や屋根の上の木も、構造上必要なものが、そのまま素直に外に現われています。床が高くなっているのは、湿気を防ぐためで、古代の農耕地帯における習慣を踏襲したものです。

▶**伊勢神宮と出雲大社**　伊勢神宮と並び、やはり古代からの土豪の神を祭った出雲大社図版 **11** は、今も二十数メートルの高さがありますが、古代では数十メートルの

the Ise Shrine is regularly rebuilt. The shrine on the right is dismantled, and a new one is built on the left. Twenty years later, the opposite process is repeated. In this way, though the shrine itself is constantly replaced, the original architectural style is faithfully passed down through history. The pattern is simply copied from the adjacent structure.

The ancient civilizations of Europe built their monuments in stone so that they would endure through the ages. And thus we still have the Greek Parthenon, Roman temples and Gothic churches.

From the beginning of recorded time the Japanese, however, built their shrines from extremely fragile, temporary materials, adopting a system of frequent reconstruction. In Japan, the emphasis was not on preserving the monument itself but preserving its form or system. So although the physical structure today may not be ancient, it is nevertheless part of an ongoing process whereby the original style can be passed on through eternity.

This concept is in many ways suggestive of today's higher technology—like computer systems in which information networks, the software, are of higher intrinsic value than the actual hardware.

As you see in the picture, the Ise Shrine features an extremely simple and functional design. There are no special adornments, and even the pillars supporting the roof and the roof beams which are structurally indispensable are left exposed without modification. The raising of the floor above ground, adopted as a countermeasure against humidity, is patterned after a similar custom in ancient agricultural regions.

▶**Izumo Shrine**   Another famous shrine dedicated to the

18 大日如来 運慶作 1176 年

Dainichi-nyorai (Mahāvairocana), by Unkei, 1176

19 十一面観音像 9世紀 Juichimen Kannon, 9th c.

大きさを持っていたと伝えられています。出雲の神は、愛と豊穣の力を支配しているとされています。

伊勢神宮をアポロ神殿にたとえるなら、出雲大社は、ヴァッカス、ディポニソス神殿といえるでしょう。この建物から、古代における技術と富の力を量(はか)ることができます。

このような神社の御霊(みたま)を分けておまつりする小さな分社が、日本のあらゆるところに作られています。これらは、街々の角やビルの谷間にも残されていますので、いつでも見ることができます。

また多くの日本人は、自分の家の棚に神社の小さな模型を作って、これらの神々をまつっています。そして自分たちの祖先の霊をまつった仏壇とともに、毎朝手を合わせ、柏手(かしわで)を打って礼拝をしてから出かけるのが、ひとつの生活習慣となっています。たましいを、活気づけ〈たまふり〉、幸いをもたらすためです。

▶**法隆寺(ほうりゅうじ)・五重の塔**　さて、**図版12**は古代・飛鳥時代の7世紀に造られた、有名な法隆寺の伽藍(がらん)です。まず、図版右側の五重の塔ですが、高さは30メートル余りで、中国・朝鮮半島から移住した技術者が伝えた仏教建築の技術を、日本的にリファインして建てられました。

たとえば、屋根の反(そ)りをみても、中国では、もっと大きく反(そ)り上がっています。それに対して日本では、ゆるやかではあるが、緊張した曲線を描いていて、日本刀の

gods of the earth since ancient days is the Izumo Shrine located in Shimane Prefecture (**Figure** 11). Although the shrine is of impressive scale today, towering some 24 meters, it is reported to have once soared nearly 100 meters in height.

The gods enshrined here are said to control the forces of love and fertile soil. If Ise Shrine were compared to the Temple of Apollo, then Izumo would correspond to the Temple of Dionysus (Bacchus). It aptly demonstrates the fine skills and abundant wealth of Japan in ancient times.

The sacred spirits enshrined in Shinto halls such as Ise and Izumo were also "distributed" in less imposing structures erected throughout the entire archipelago. Even today these small shrines can still be seen on local street corners and in lonely valleys tucked between large buildings.

Many people also continue to enshrine these same gods in small shrine replicas which they set on a high shelf in their home. It remains customary for many Japanese to leave for work in the morning only after they have brought their hands together in prayer before the deities, in addition to prayers before a Buddhist altar dedicated to the spirits of their ancestors. Such actions are said to bring spiritual vitality and happiness.

▶ **The five-storied pagoda** Figure 12 is a picture of Horyuji, a famous Buddhist temple located near Nara and dating to the Asuka period (7th century). In the right portion of the figure we see the temple's five-storied pagoda. It stands more than 30 meters tall and was built based on Buddhist architectural techniques transmitted from China and the Korean peninsula.

To these basic techniques were added Japanese refinements, such as the restrained curving of the roof compared with

21 厳島　海に浮かぶ神社

Itsukushima: a floating shrine

20 京都御所 清涼殿(せいりょうでん)

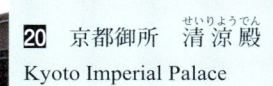

Kyoto Imperial Palace

反りと共通の曲線だと言われています。また、屋根を支える支柱の作り出すデザインは、力学的な必要性から生まれたもので、いわゆる20世紀の機能主義的な美しさを、すでに充分に表わしています。

　また、驚くべきことに、この木造の五重の塔は、日本を襲った多くの地震にも壊れ倒れることがありませんでした。なぜなら、この建築はいわゆる柔構造になっているからです。屋根の中心から建物の一番底まで、一本の柱が下がっていますが、それが固定されないで、自由に動きます。

　つまり地震の時に建物と反対側にその中心の柱が動いて、いくら揺れても柔らかく曲がるだけで、かえって崩れることがありません。今日の高層建築を支える柔構造の考え方とまったく同じです。

▶寺院建築の三大要素　一般に日本の仏教寺院は、塔、金堂(こんどう)、そして講堂という三つの要素から成り立っています。これに付属して、鐘楼(しょうろう)、経蔵(きょうぞう)が左右に、そして奥の方に、僧侶の生活する僧坊と、食事をする食堂(じきどう)、洗面所である東司(とうす)があるのがふつうです。

　では、寺院に必ずある塔は、何をシンボルするのでしょう。実は、塔は釈迦牟尼(しゃかむに)——シッダルタのお墓の印でした。インドではストゥーパといわれ、円形の丘でしたが、中国、韓国、日本へ伝わるにしたがって、このような美しい塔になったわけです。

Chinese precedents. The Japanese-style curve is more gentle while still retaining a sense of tension, much in the manner of the traditional Japanese sword. The design created by the pillars supporting the roof—which actually evolved from the requirements of dynamics—conveys a functional beauty which is surprisingly modern.

Equally surprising is the fact that this wooden pagoda has survived thirteen centuries and numerous earthquakes. This durability derives from the pagoda's "flexible" structure in which the central pillar hangs free from the roof toward the ground, not fixed in place.

During an earthquake the pillar moves in the opposite direction from the rest of the structure. No matter how strong the tremor, the pagoda merely bends but will not topple. This principle is exactly the same as that which is incorporated today in the construction of giant skyscrapers.

▶**Main elements of Buddhist temples**　In Japan, Buddhist temples normally consist of three main elements: the pagoda, the *kondo* or main hall, and the *kodo* or lecture hall. These are usually supported by lesser structures including the bell tower and sutra repository to the left and right, as well as amenities for the resident monks (dormitories, dining hall and latrine) located at the rear.

What do pagodas, this omnipresent fixture of Buddhist temples, symbolize? In origin they represented the burial grave of Sākyamuni, i.e. Siddhartha Gautama, the founder of Buddhism. In India, the earliest structures of this kind are round in shape and known as stupas.

They went through various transformations when Buddhism passed into Japan through China and Korea, finally settling in the attractive form of the pagoda as we know it.

22 平等院　鳳凰堂　11世紀
Hoo-do (Phoenix Hall), Byodoin Temple, 11th c.

23 鳳凰堂の内部　11世紀

Interior, Hoo-do, 11th c.

法隆寺では、塔に並んで金堂が建っています。**図版⓬**の左側の建物です。この建物の中には仏像が置かれ、壁画が描かれていて、釈迦牟尼の説いた仏法の世界が、この建物によって象徴されています。

　図版⓭が、その壁画の一部です。この阿弥陀浄土のイメージ図のなかに描かれた観音菩薩像は、きわめて美しく、またインドのアジャンタ石窟寺院に、ほとんど同じ像が描かれていることでも有名です。

▶**女性の理想像**　**図版⓮**は法隆寺に隣接する寺院、中宮寺の弥勒菩薩像で、高さ1.3メートルのものです。お顔はひじょうに美しく、ここに見られる誇張のない優しさは、インドや中国の仏像には見られないもので、日本の女性の理想像を表わしています。肩の線の流れ、胴のくり方、膝の膨らみなど、プリミティブで単純化されてはいますが、われわれに、人間的であたたかい感動を与えてくれます。

　一般に美術というものは、すべてに言えることですが、全体のプロポーションとそれを生かすディテールの美しさ、つまり細かい部分の完成度によって、芸術としての価値が定まります。逆にいえば、当時の人々の感性のレベルを知ることができます。

　一般に日本の仏像は、写実的ではありませんが、現世的であたたかく、人間に親しみやすいものとなっています。

At Horyuji, the pagoda stands adjacent to the main hall, the building seen at the left in **Figure 12**. The main hall contains Buddhist images and wall paintings which vividly depict the world of Buddhist scripture as preached by Sākyamuni.

Figure 13 shows part of these wall paintings, an artistic rendering of the Pure Land of Amida Buddha. Here we see the image of Kannon, Goddess of Mercy (Avalokiteśvara), depicted with exquisite beauty. A very similar image can be found in the cave temples of Ajanta in India.

▶**The ideal of femininity** **Figure 14** is a picture of a statue of the bodhisattva Miroku (Maitreya) located at Chuguji Temple close to Horyuji. Standing 1.3 meters, the statue is graced with a face of exceptional beauty, and gentility of a degree unknown in the Buddhist statuary of India or China. Indeed, it embodies the ideal of Japanese femininity. Features such as the lines of the shoulders, the curves of the torso and the rounded fullness of the knees, though here simplified in a primitive style, emanate an unmistakable feeling of warmth and emotion.

Generally speaking, all forms of art are accorded artistic value based on the beauty of their total proportions and the degree of detailed perfection which make such proportions come to life. By extension, these points also enable us to know the level of sensitivity demonstrated by those who lived in the age in which such works were created. Japan's Buddhist imagery for the most part, though not realistic, exudes a warm sense of earthliness, warmth which engenders human sympathy.

24 源氏物語絵巻　柏木(かしわぎ)の段　12世紀

Scene from *The Tale of Genji* scrolls, 12th c.

25 鳥獣戯画絵巻　12世紀

Monochrome animal caricatures, 12th c.

▶**凍れる音楽**　図版**16**は、奈良にあるこれもまた有名な薬師寺の三重の塔です。高さ34メートルで、8世紀のはじめに造られています。六層に見えますけれども、実際は三層です。というのは、それぞれの階に、裳階というスカートのようなものがついているわけです。

しかし、この屋根と裳階との繰り返しによって大きさの変化が生まれ、人々はここに音楽的なリズムの美しさを感じることができます。この塔を評して、一種の〈凍れる音楽〉であると言った人もいるほどです。このような変化に富んだ美しさを、実に8世紀の建築家は、すでに造っていたわけです。

また、この塔の構造は、先ほどの法隆寺に比べると、さらにひじょうに細かくデリケートで軽やかさを表わしています。大陸から入った仏教建築が、日本的な観点によって、しだいに洗練されていったことが分かります。

▶**菩薩の表現**　このお寺の東院という建物に、本尊として聖観音菩薩像がまつられています（**図版15**）。この「菩薩」というのは、人間が仏、すなわち真理に達する過程での中間段階にあって、あと一歩で悟りに達する状態の人をいいます。造型においては、インド風の装飾をつけているのが特徴です。仏に達してしまいますと、真理そのものですから、このような装飾品をつけることはありません。

この菩薩像は、顔も体もひじょうに引き締まった若い

▶**Frozen music**　Figure **16** shows another famous pagoda, the three-storied pagoda of Yakushiji Temple in Nara. Rising 34 meters skyward, this structure was erected in the beginning of the 8th century. It appears to have six stories but in reality has only three. The illusion is created by the addition of a skirt known as a *mokoshi* on each story.

The alternation of the roofs and mokoshi makes for variations in size which impress the viewer in a manner resembling musical undulations. In fact, the effect has been referred to as "music frozen in time." Even as far back as the 8th century, architects were already capable of creating beauty of such varied splendor.

The 8th-century pagoda of Yakushiji also gives an impression of delicacy and lightness far exceeding that of the 7th-century Horyuji pagoda introduced earlier. From this fact we see that Buddhist architecture, of continental origins, was gradually refined according to Japanese tastes and sensibilities.

▶**The bodhisattva**　The Toindo, or East Hall, of Yakushiji preserves as its main icon an image of the bodhisattva Sho Kannon (Arya Avalokiteśvara, Figure **15**). A bodhisattva is a human being in a state of existence just one step before enlightenment and Buddhahood. Bodhisattvas are artistically recognizable by their Indian-style adornment. This adornment is not found on images depicting Buddhas who have already attained the state of enlightenment.

The Sho Kannon which we see here appears to be a young man with a muscled countenance and well-formed physique which together radiate a spirit of great strength.

The Nara period which gave birth to the structures and images introduced so far lasted approximately eighty years

27 扇面法華経冊子　12世紀

Fan-shaped album of the *Lotus Sutra*, 12th c.

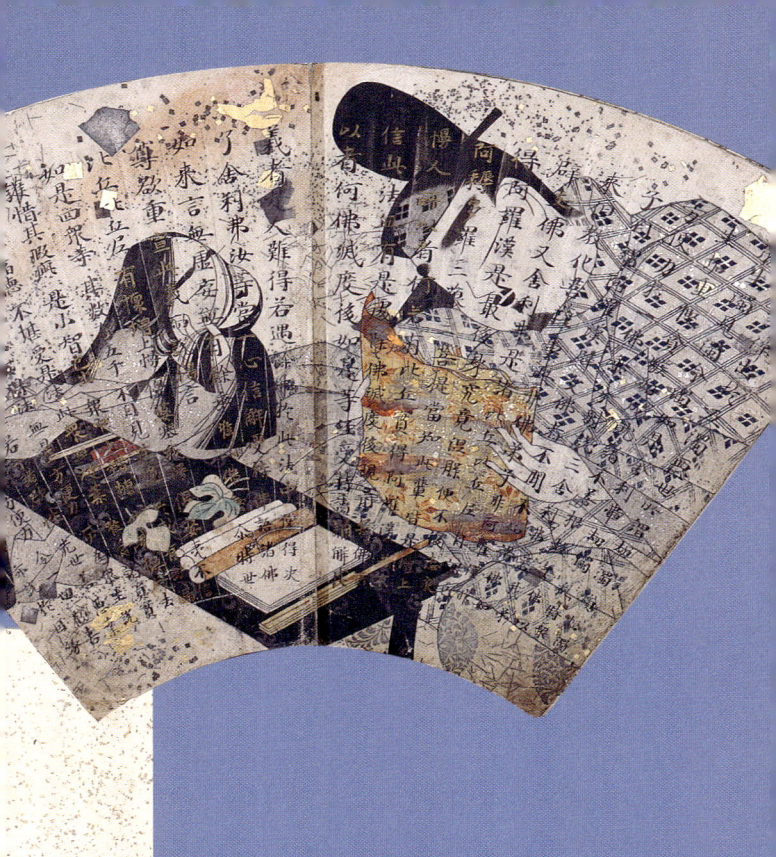

26　三十六人家集　能宣集　12世紀
Anthology of the Thirty-six Poets, 12th c.

青年の姿を思わせるもので、力に満ちた精神を表現していると言えます。

さて、このような建物・仏像を造った奈良時代は、ほぼ7代の天皇の統治する80年間続き、その後、都は京都へと移りました。

▶**天皇の宮殿**　図版**20**は、京都に残る、当時の天皇の宮殿です。建物自体は19世紀に建て替えられたものですが、創建当時の形式を伝えるものです。ひじょうに清潔でシンプルな感じがします。平安時代は、中国の文化や制度が大量に取り入れられた時代ですが、天皇の宮殿が、伊勢神宮と同じように、白木の木造平屋で造られ、屋根も木の皮を重ねた檜皮葺きとなっているのは、注目すべきことです。けばけばしい彩色も施されてはいません。太い列柱がギリシャ神殿のように連なり、単純で機能的な構造を示しています。明るく明快で、自然に向かって解放された空間が演出され、清潔を尊ぶ伝統が流れています。

▶**地上の極楽浄土**　図版**22**は同時代に造られた貴族・藤原頼通の別荘ですが、きわめて中国的な装飾が施されています。彼はここに仏をまつり、この仏殿を中心にした庭園寺院を造りました。京都の南、宇治川に臨む平等院の鳳凰堂です。

この建物は、天国にいる想像上の鳥が翼をひろげたデ

through the reigns of seven emperors. It then came to a close with the relocation of the capital in A.D. 794 to Heian, more familiarly known as Kyoto.

▶ **Imperial Palace**   Figure **20** shows the Imperial Palace in Kyoto. Although the present structure dates only to the 19th century, it wholly retains the style of the Heian period of the 11th and 12th centuries, a style of extreme purity and simplicity.

At the time, Chinese cultural and political systems were being adopted in great measure by the Heian court. As we see here, in building their new Imperial Palace the Japanese leaders chose a native style of architecture like that seen in the Ise Shrine: a single-storied structure of unpainted wood, free of all exterior coloration and topped by a multi-layered thatched roof of cypress bark.

The palace's colonnade, both simple and functional in design, stretches majestically like the columns of a Greek temple. The total effect created by the structure is that of a bright, spacious area opening out toward nature and blended with a traditional respect for pristine neatness.

▶ **An earthly paradise**   In Figure **22** we see the Hoo-do, or Phoenix Hall, of the Byodoin Temple located on the banks of the Uji River south of Kyoto. Constructed about the same time as the Kyoto Imperial Palace, this building was originally built as a villa for Fujiwara no Yorimichi (992-1074), a powerful member of the Kyoto aristocracy. It is decorated in a style which shows strong Chinese influences. Yorimichi enshrined a statue of Amida Buddha here and developed the site into a Buddhist temple with lavish gardens centered on the main hall.

28 伝源頼朝像　12世紀

Portrait of Minamoto no Yoritomo, 12th c.

29 明恵上人像　13世紀

Portrait of Myoe, 13th c.

ザインをかたどっています。周囲の庭園は、経典に描かれたとおりに造られ、死後行くであろうパラダイスを、この地上にそっくり造り出すよう意図されています。当時の人々は、現世でこの庭園と建物を眺めることによって、死後、極楽浄土へ行けるというきわめて現実的な信仰を持っていました。

　この庭はまた、浄土式といわれる日本の庭園の原形ともなっています。ここでは、庭を単に生活を楽しむ道具としてではなく、日常生活を超えた理想の世界として、表現しようという気持ちが見られます。このように日本の庭園は、自然を再現することによって、自然の法則、つまり精神的真実をより明らかにすることにつとめてきました。

▶**阿弥陀さま**　鳳凰堂の堂内には大きな阿弥陀仏の像があり、さまざまな室内装飾が施されています（**図版23**）。朝、光がここに差しますと、その光が阿弥陀さまのお顔を照らし、まわりの壁は光を反射して、あたかも光の中にいるような、居ながらにして極楽浄土にいるかのような深い感動に襲われたと言われています。また、夕方になると、西の光が池に反射して堂の中を照らしました。

　ここで見られるとおり、日本の住宅も、寺院も、自然との関係がきわめて重要です。鳳凰堂の前に見える池は、実は宇治川につながっていました。人々は船に乗っ

Viewed from above, Phoenix Hall is designed to suggest an imaginary bird in heaven spreading its wings. Its gardens were built in the image described in the Buddhist scriptures, to serve as an earthly imitation of the Buddhist conception of paradise.

People at that time believed that if they viewed this building and its surrounding gardens on earth, they would be able to go to the Pure Land of Buddhist paradise after death. Consequently, the gardens came to serve as the precursor of the so-called "Pure Land" style Japanese garden. In this way, the gardens of the Byodoin are meant to be more than a venue of recreational enjoyment; they were also meant to serve as a symbol of an ideal world transcending mortal matters. The Japanese garden thus sought to recreate nature as a way of clarifying the laws of nature relating to spiritual truth.

▶**Amida Buddha**　Inside, the hall features a large statue of Amida Buddha and various interior decorations (**Figure 23**). When the morning sun shines, it radiates directly on the Buddha's countenance and is reflected off the surrounding walls, creating a deeply moving scene in which the visitor has the sensation of being in paradise. A similar emotional wonder is to be enjoyed when the setting sun is reflected off the pond into the interior.

Like Japanese homes, in temples too the relationship with nature is an important element. Originally the pond in front of Phoenix Hall, for example, was actually joined with the Uji River, and visitors were able to reach the temple by boat. Also, the building itself faces east, meaning that prayers are offered facing west, which, according to Buddhist beliefs, is the direction of the Pure Land where souls transmigrate.

30 一遍上人絵伝　13世紀

"A Pictorial Biography of Monk Ippen," painted scroll, 13th c.

31 三十三間堂　千体千手観音像　13世紀
Thousand statues of Senju Kannon, Sanjusangendo Hall, 13th c.

て川からここを訪れ、参ることができました。

　また、この建物は東を向いていますから、このお堂を拝(おが)む人は、西に向かって拝むことになります。日本では、死者は西方にある浄土へゆくと考えられています。特に西の山といいますと、仏教が日本に伝わる以前から、死者の行くべき国があると考えられていたのです。今でも亡くなった人は、頭を北にして西の方向に向けて寝かせる習慣があります。

▶海の中の別荘　図版 **21** は瀬戸内海にある厳島(いつくしま)神社です。時は12世紀。貴族社会が終わりに近づき、平家と源氏という二つの大きな豪族が権力の座を争った時代ですが、この建築は、瀬戸内海という海の中に建てられた平家の別荘を、後に神社にしたものです。同時に、中国や朝鮮半島の外交官を迎える迎賓館(げいひんかん)としての役割も果たしていました。

　したがって、これは神社ではありますが、当時の貴族の住まいを表現しています。自然の秩序のなかに置かれ、海そのものを大きな中庭として取り入れています。建物を長い渡り廊下がつなぎ、大いなる海の自然に溶け込むような環境を形づくっています。全体に水平線によって強く印象づけられます。

　厳島神社の場合は海ですが、当時の貴族の住まいは、多くの場合、建物のまわりに池が造られています。一般に寝殿造りといわれますが、注目すべきことは、さまざ

In Japan, this concept that the dead go to a land in the west actually predates the arrival of Buddhism, and early literature refers to this afterworld as "the western mountain." Even today, it is customary to lay the dead to rest facing west.

▶**Villa in the sea** Figure **21** shows the Itsukushima Shrine of Miyajima, a Shinto shrine built in the Seto Inland Sea in the 12th century. The shrine was originally constructed as a villa of the Taira clan, one of the two major aristocratic clans of the Heian period (the other being the Minamoto), and also served as an official guesthouse to welcome diplomats from China and the Korean peninsula.

In spite of its present religious role, therefore, the structure represents a well-preserved example of an aristocratic residence of its period—a style known as *shinden-zukuri*.

As we see, it is picturesquely set amid the well-ordered backdrop of nature, the sea serving as its private garden. Long corridors connect the various buildings to create an extremely pleasant environment in which man-made structures blend harmoniously into their natural setting, accented by the distant horizon.

While the Itsukushima Shrine is set directly in the sea, in most shinden-zukuri architecture of the period a corresponding visual effect is created by an artificial pond. The gardens surrounding the pond were used for parties and other everyday recreations.

The buildings themselves functioned only as points from which to view such activities, or merely as sleeping quarters. Amid this setting, boats were floated to the accompaniment of music, poetry exchanges were held, and wine flowed freely.

32　金閣と庭園　14世紀創建

Kinkaku (Golden Pavilion) and garden, orig. 14th c.

33 銀閣　15 世紀
Ginkaku (Silver Pavilion), 15th c.

まな生活やパーティなどがこの池をめぐる庭園で行なわれ、建物はそれを眺める場所、あるいは寝るだけの場所に過ぎなかったということです。その池に舟を浮かべて音楽を奏し、詩の贈答をしたり酒宴をひらいたりしたのです。

　今日でも、この厳島神社では、毎年1回、大潮(おおしお)がくる祭礼の日に、神の神輿(みこし)が対岸のお旅所(たびしょ)まで、海を渡って往復するというお祭りが行なわれています。神輿を宮廷風の舟に乗せ、十数人の女装の漕ぎ手が、太鼓に合わせて漕いでゆきました。管絃祭(かんげんさい)と呼ばれているように、平安時代の管絃を鳴らし、衣裳を着けて、ひじょうに華やかなものです。

▶『源氏物語』の世界　時代はやや遡(さかのぼ)りますが、そのような平安時代の貴族の暮らしを書いた長編小説に、有名な『源氏物語』があります。いくつもの翻訳が出ていますが、世界でも指折りの大長編小説の一つで、そこには、宮廷に生活する男女の間に展開する、近代的ともいうべき細やかな心理描写がみられます。

　またその一方で、日本の古代からの伝統的な自然観、つまり、四季の移り変わりのなかに自らの運命を映して読み取る自然観が綯(な)い交ぜられた、奇跡的な傑作です。日本でも、以来、これ以上の長編小説は書かれていませんが、世界でもマルセル・プルーストの長編に比較されるひじょうに高級な大長編です。

Even today a festival is held at the Itsukushima Shrine once a year at the time of highest tide. During the festival a *mikoshi*, or sacred shrine palanquin, is carried across the sea and back in a boat of ancient court style rowed to the beat of a drum by a dozen or so men. Known as "Kangen-sai," or the "Festival of Wind and String Music," the celebration is a lavish and festive affair marked by the playing of music and wearing of costumes dating to the Heian period.

▶ ***The Tale of Genji*** The lifestyle of the Heian aristocracy is vividly documented in *The Tale of Genji*, a work of fiction written in the 11th century. In this novel of extraordinary length, which has been translated into numerous foreign languages, the everyday lives of the court aristocracy are described in psychological detail of almost uncanny "modernity."

Yet at the same time, tradition is faithfully preserved in the portrayal of characters who contemplate their fate in terms of the vicissitudes of nature, in the context of the changing seasons, just as the ancients did. It is this striking dichotomy—its modernity juxtaposed with its steeped traditions—that makes *The Tale of Genji* such a miraculous literary achievement.

No novel of comparable length and depth was ever written in Japan again, and it easily ranks on a par with the epoch-making fictional monument of Marcel Proust.

At the time of its writing, *The Tale of Genji* and other fictional tales comprised a literary genre enjoyed only by the distaff members of the aristocracy. Works such as these were not actually read by the ranking court ladies. Instead their

34 西芳寺庭園　洪隠山石組　14世紀
"Koinzan" rock formation, Saihoji Temple, 14th c.

35 大仙院庭園　**16世紀**

Stone garden, Daisen-in Monastery,
Daitokuji Temple, 16th c.

さて、当時は、物語を目で読むのではなく、女主人に絵を見せながらお付きの者が物語を読んで聞かせ、それを宮廷の女性たちが一緒に楽しむという味わい方をしました。先にも述べたとおり、ここでも個人ではなく、みんなで一つの物語を楽しむという形が採られていました。

　図版 24 は、源氏物語が作られてからおよそ 100 年ほど後の 12 世紀に作られた源氏物語絵巻です。絵巻というのは日本独特の絵画のジャンルであり、このような画面と、ストーリーを書いた文字の部分とが交互に現われ、絵と文章と両方でストーリーが展開していきます。逆に言えば、絵と文字とが一体になっているわけです。もっとも、今日のテレビジョンや映画のことを考えれば別に不思議はありません。

▶**日本人の個性描写**　ここにあげた図は、ひじょうに有名な場面で、貴族の女性と男性が描かれています。女性は、十二単衣と言われるひじょうに豪華な着物を着ています。顔の描写が単純化されており、〈ひき目・かぎ鼻〉といわれるいかにもティピカル（類型的）な表現です。

　そのため個性が現われていないという非難を受けるかもしれませんが、それは日本文化の常として、個人に中心を置くのではなく、全体のシチュエーションに中心を置いて描かれているためです。

courtiers would read the stories aloud to them as they gathered together and viewed illustrations which provided visual enhancement. In this way, the enjoyment of literature was a collaborative and collective affair.

Figure **24** shows part of the *emaki*, or illustrated handscrolls, used with *The Tale of Genji*. They date to the 12th century, some one hundred years after the novel itself was written. Emaki such as these constitute a genre of art unique to Japan, a genre in which pictures and words are featured on the same scrolls to tell a story.

The emaki is thus a work which simultaneously contains elements of both art and literature. This combination is by no means exceptional, of course, when we note the inherent similarity with today's television and movies.

▶**Simplification of individual characterization**   The scene from *Genji* depicted in the accompanying figure is extremely famous. It shows ladies and men of the aristocracy. The women are dressed in sumptuous, many-layered kimonos known as *juni-hitoe*. Their facial features are greatly simplified using a stereotypical technique known as *hikime-kagibana*, "line-for-an-eye, hook-for-a-nose."

Although this form of artistic expression might be criticized for its failure to convey individual characterization, the preference for such a style is a manifestation of Japan's enduring culture that has always emphasized the entire situation rather than one specific individual.

A similar circumstance exists in Kabuki, a theatrical form whose stories are generally understood only by those in the audience who bring with them considerable knowledge on the subject. Just the same, this inability to follow the complete

36 天橋立図　雪舟筆　16世紀

"View of Amanohashidate," by Sesshu, 16th c.

37 那智滝図 13世紀 "Nachi Waterfall," 13th c.

たとえば歌舞伎ですが、日本人でもよほど詳しい人以外は、ストーリーはよくわかりません。しかし、全体のストーリーを追わなくても、部分部分のデザイン、踊りとのコンストラクション、またはドラマのシチュエーションに深い感動を味わうことができます。

▶**経典の筆写**　図版 27 はいわゆる扇です。もともとは暑いときに風を送るための扇に、仏教の経典を書いたものです。日本では、このように、扇に詩や経典を書くことが、たいへん多く行なわれました。貴族は経典を写すことによってご利益(りやく)が得られると考えたので、ひじょうに美しい経典の筆写をいくつも作りました。ここに挙げたのは聖徳太子の寺・四天王寺(してんのうじ)に十数枚残されたもののうちの一枚です。ひじょうに見事な絵が描かれていて、経典というよりも、ほとんど美術品のように見えます。信仰生活さえも、一つの美的な生活にしてしまわねば気がすまない日本の貴族たちの生活心情が、よく現われています。

▶**書道の楽しみ**　同じように、日本では文字を書くことそれ自体も、一つの芸術としてたいへん尊重されました。書(しょ)、または書道といいますが、今日でもご年輩の方の多くは、墨と毛筆で字を書くことができますし、現に習っている人も大勢います。それを晩年の楽しみにするということが、いまも行なわれているわけです。

story does not prevent an audience from being deeply moved by the stage settings, the dancing or the overall drama that unfolds before them.

▶**Buddhist sutras on fans**   Figure **27** looks like a fan but is actually a fan-shaped album of Buddhist sutras. In Japan it was quite common to write poetry or Buddhist sutras on real fans. The aristocracy believed that copying scripture would bring them divine favor, and as a result they produced many sutras of great beauty.

The album depicted here is one of a dozen or so passed down through the ages at Shitennoji, a temple in Osaka founded by Prince Shotoku in the 6th century. So exceptional is their beauty that, rather than works of scripture, they are better appreciated as works of art. They vividly exemplify the everyday attitude of the ancient aristocracy—an attitude marked by an intrinsic compulsion, even in their acts of religious faith, to create a world of artistic beauty.

▶**Calligraphy**   In the same way, the writing of characters itself—calligraphy—was traditionally elevated to a fine art. Even today, most Japanese over the age of 50 are able to write with ink and brush, and calligraphy lessons continue to win a strong following. Many turn to calligraphy as a pastime in their retirement years.

The people of the Heian period also infused elaborate innovations into the paper which they used for calligraphy. The example seen in **Figure 26** shows a waka poem inscribed on specially patterned paper. Today it is designated a National Treasure.

38　能面　孫次郎　16世紀
"Magojiro" Noh Mask, 16th c.

39 西本願寺　北能舞台　16世紀

North Noh stage, Nishi-Honganji Temple, 16th c.

当時の人々は、字を書く紙もひじょうに工夫しました。**図版 26** の作品の場合は、地紋(じもん)のある紙に和歌を書いたもので、国宝となっています。

3. 中世の世界 （鎌倉・室町・桃山時代）

▶**日本の肖像画**　**図版 28** は、はじめて鎌倉に幕府を開いた将軍・源 頼朝(みなもとのよりとも)（1147〜99年）の像で、12世紀の末に描かれたものです。日本では、一般に肖像画というジャンルはありません。なぜなら、何度か述べたように、日本では一人の人間の個性や性格を描くよりも、その人物の背後にある精神的なものを描こうとしたからです。目の前の人物は、目に見えない魂の仮の姿にすぎないと考えるのです。

　フランスの大臣で、作家・美術評論家でもあったアンドレ・マルローは、この絵を見て、「世界で最もすぐれた人物画のひとつである。なぜなら、画面全体を区切る黒い線、鋭い形と全体のバランスといったものが、単なる人物以上のものを表現しているからだ」と述べています。20世紀の最も先端を行く美術批評家が、このような日本の古い絵画に共感を覚えたということは、たいへん興味深いことです。

▶**坐禅の明恵上人(みょうえ)**　**図版 29** は、先に「あかあかや」と月の光をうたった詩の作者として紹介した、明恵上人(みょうえしょうにん)（1173〜1232年）の肖像です。彼は、このように自然

3. The Middle Ages
    (Kamakura, Muromachi, Momoyama)

▶**Japanese portraiture**　Figure 28 is a portrait painting of Minamoto no Yoritomo (1147-99), founder of the Kamakura Shogunate. The existence of such a portrait, which dates to the late 12th century, is highly unusual.

As I indicated earlier, the Japanese tended to focus on a person's inspirational forces rather than on his individual traits or personality. A flesh-and-blood human being was interpreted as nothing more than a temporary embodiment of an invisible spirit.

The great French statesman, author and art critic André Malraux (1901-76) hailed this Japanese work as one of the most outstanding portrait paintings in the world. He praised its overall composition, the striking visual effect of its black lines and the resulting sense of balanced proportion, applauding the portrait as an artistic expression that transcends mere physical description. It is extremely interesting to note that one of the 20th century's most avant-garde art critics would so appreciate a Japanese painting of such antiquity.

▶**Myoe in meditation**　Figure 29 is a portrait of Myoe, the Buddhist monk cited earlier for his unconventional poem on moonlight ("How bright!..."). As it shows, Myoe habitually meditated in tranquil solitude off in the mountains.

In the painting Myoe is seen perched in the forked limbs of a tree. Birds appear to his upper right, and a squirrel frolics near him as if with great familiarity.

The painting naturally portrays a likeness of Myoe the man, yet it is more than just a portrait. It is cherished (and designated a National Treasure) for its convincing depiction of Myoe at one with his natural surroundings, deep in meditation.

40 檜図屏風　狩野永徳筆　16世紀

"Japanese Cypress," by Kano Eitoku, 16th c.

の山の中に一人分け入り、静かに坐禅をしました。この絵では、上人は木の股のところで坐禅をしています。画面の右上には鳥が見えます。ほかにもリスなどの小動物がいて、たいへん親しみを持って上人のそばに集まってきているのが見られます。

　画面に描かれた上人の顔は、もちろん、実際の上人の顔と似せられていますが、この絵の場合でも単に肖像画というのではなく、坐禅を組んで瞑想（めいそう）にふけっている彼の生活、その背景にある自然との一体感を描いたものとしてとらえられ、礼拝されています。もちろん、国宝です。

▶一遍（いっぺん）上人の念仏　図版 30 は、武家出身の念仏行者・一遍（いっぺん）上人（1239～89年）の絵巻です。彼は13世紀の大衆的な宗教家で、中世にあって熱狂的な信者を集めました。彼の周辺には、数十人、数百人の人々が集まり、念仏を称（とな）えながら踊り狂ったのです。

　中世の武士たちは、戦いによって常に死と直面していました。飢餓や疫病（しっぺい）もはやっていたので、宗教は次第に貴族のものから武士のものへ、個人のものへと広がっていったのです。それだけに、いま、念仏によって救われるという教えは、彼らをとらえました。

　図は、やぐらの上で念仏踊りを踊っている場面です。金鼓（きんこ）を鳴らして踊りを踊る。ここでの踊りは、宗教的なエクスタシーの表現としての踊りです。身分の低いもの

▶**Emaki of Ippen**   Figure **30** is an emaki scroll painting of Ippen (1239-89), a Buddhist monk of samurai background who renounced the world and became an itinerant preacher of the saving grace which could be reaped through continuous recitation of the name of Amitabha (Amida) Buddha.

Ippen succeeded in attracting a huge following of ardent believers among the common masses during the 13th century. Hundreds would gather around him to intone the name of Buddha and dance into an ecstatic frenzy.

The Middle Ages were a period when samurai warriors constantly faced the prospect of death in battle, while the masses were continually confronted with rampant starvation and pestilence. Under these influences, religion gradually spread from its earlier embracement by the aristocracy to include the warrior class and the common man, among whom the concept of salvation through recitation of Buddha's name took hold rapidly and firmly.

The painting shows one such "dance of intonement" being performed at a temple. In religious ecstasy, the participants would gyrate wildly to the beat of drums and everyone, aristocrat and commoner alike, danced together without distinction. Ippen dedicated his whole life to saving the common man in this manner, choosing to walk the length and breadth of Japan preaching rather than seeking to erect temples of magnificent splendor.

In the end, however, he died without a successor to carry on his mission. More than all else, he valued the intonation of the Buddha's name in a spirit of unsullied spiritual purity, and although he was a Buddhist priest he often visited Shinto shrines because to Ippen they represented the essence of unadorned piety. Ippen thereby played an important role in the Japanization of the Buddhist religion.

41 松本城　天守　16世紀
Matsumoto Castle, 16th c.

42 茶室待庵の内部　16世紀

Interior of Taian teahouse, 16th c.

から貴族に至るまで、区別なく踊っています。

　一遍は立派な寺院を造ることよりも、このように、直接、庶民を救うことを目的として日本国中を歩きつづけ、ついに後継者を作らぬまま亡くなっていきました。彼は、白木の念仏、つまり、純粋無垢な雑念のない念仏こそ最高のものと考え、僧侶でありながら、いつも神社におまいりをしていました。仏教を日本化した人といえます。

▶**金閣と銀閣**　図版**32**は京都を旅する人が一度は訪れる、有名な金閣寺です。文字どおり金箔が張ってあるので、金閣と言われました。将軍・足利義満（1358〜1408年）の別邸として造られたものですが、一階は日本の住居の伝統を引いた書院造りで、上の階は仏教の建物を採り入れていて、それを見事に一体化しております。

　義満は、中国貿易を独占して巨額な富と権力を手にし、その資金でこの絢爛豪華な建物を造ったわけです。

　義満の孫の義政（1436〜90年）は、これを一層洗練して日本的にしようと考え、京の東山に銀閣という別荘を建てました（図版**33**）。名前は銀閣ですが、銀は張ってありません。むしろ池や庭園・枯山水の石組みなどがすぐれ、控えめな美しさを出そうとしております。

　義政は、この自然に溶けこんだ風景の中で、茶の湯を行ないました。彼は時の将軍でありながら政治から離

▶**Golden and silver pavilions**　Figure **32** is Kinkaku, the famed "Golden Pavilion" in Kyoto so called because of its gold-leaf gilding. It was originally constructed as a villa of the third Muromachi Shogun, Ashikaga Yoshimitsu (1358-1408), who built it using vast riches he had amassed through his monopoly on trade with China.

The shimmeringly beautiful structure represents a brilliant mingling of two unique architectural styles. The first story is constructed in the *shoin-zukuri* motif based on traditional domestic architecture, while the upper two stories incorporate features of Buddhist architecture.

Ashikaga Yoshimasa (1436-90), Yoshimitsu's grandson and likewise a ruling Shogun, later followed in his grandfather's footsteps by building his own retreat in the scenic Higashiyama area of Kyoto. In keeping with his tastes Yoshimasa sought a more refined, more "Japanese" structure that was ultimately named Ginkaku, the "Silver Pavilion" (**Figure 33**).

The name notwithstanding, Ginkaku is not gilded in silver. Quite the contrary, instead of a glittery display of wealth such as that seen in Kinkaku, Ginkaku was designed to create an aura of restrained beauty through the use of a pond and gardens, including austere "gardens" of rock and sand. Yoshimasa eventually withdrew from political life and passed his days here serenely engaged in pastimes of an artistic nature, often using his elegant setting as a backdrop for the tea ceremony.

As early as the 15th century, Ginkaku and its gardens served as architectural harbingers of the dwellings and gardens of modern Japan.

43 志野茶碗　銘「卯花墻」　16世紀
"Unohanagaki" Shino style tea bowl, 16th c.

44 黒楽茶碗
銘「あやめ」
長次郎作
16世紀
"Ayame" Raku ware tea bowl, by Chojiro, 16th c.

45 伊賀水指
銘「破袋」 16世紀
"Yaburebukuro" water jar, Iga ware, 16th c.

46 花入　銘「園城寺」 16世紀
"Onjoji" flower vase, by Sen no Rikyu, 16th c.

れ、ひたすら趣味的で美的な生活に没頭して、生涯を過ごしたのです。

ここで見られる建物と庭園には、すでに現代の日本人の、住宅と庭園の原型が見られます。15世紀のことです。

▶日本の庭園とは　一般に日本の庭園は、自然を自然のままに、または、自然をより一層自然らしく見せるために石や木を配置します。これに対してヨーロッパやイスラムの庭園は、幾何学的で人間精神の秩序を表現しようとするものです。

またヨーロッパの庭園は、建物に付属するものですが、日本の場合は、むしろ庭園が主であって、その自然の中に宇宙の真実があり、その中の一つの風景として建物を置くという考え方に立ちます。したがって、庭園はひじょうに重要なものです。

もちろん、樹木はしだいに変化していくものです。したがって、人は庭園を造ったとき、少なくとも5年、ときには50年、100年たってはじめて、その美しさが現われると考えています。つまり、人間がすべてを造るのではなく、自然の力によって庭が造られていく、人間はその自然に手を貸すだけである、と考えるのです。

▶苔の庭の美しさ　実は、銀閣寺や金閣寺のさらに原型となった建物と庭園がありました。今、その建物は残っ

▶**Japanese gardens** Generally speaking, the Japanese garden is designed to show off nature as it exists. At times, however, rocks and trees are added in an artificial arrangement aimed at "improving" on nature by rendering it "more natural." In traditional European and Islamic cultures, gardens adopted geometric patterns which expressed the order of the human spirit.

In Europe, a garden was also viewed as an appendage to a building, playing a sort of supporting role. This is in direct contrast to the Japanese garden, which is always given the leading role in the architectural drama. In Japan, a garden and its natural elements contain cosmic truths, and any buildings which are present serve merely as fixtures of the overall setting. In all cases, it is the garden which is of foremost importance.

Trees of course undergo gradual change as they grow. It is commonly understood that a Japanese garden reaches its full bloom of beauty at least five years after it is completed, and sometimes even fifty or one hundred years later. In this respect, it is not man who creates the garden, but nature. Man merely lends a helping hand.

▶**A natural carpet of moss** Both Kinkaku and Ginkaku were actually preceded by another structure and garden which served as the model for these famed sites. Though the structure is no longer there, the garden is, and it is one of the more popular attractions in Kyoto. The garden I refer to is that of Saihoji Temple, more commonly known as Kokedera, or "Moss Temple."

The structure at Saihoji was an ornate, two-storied edifice called Ruriden, or "Palace of Lapis Lazuli." After it was devastated by fire, the site was abandoned for several centuries

47 東照宮　陽明門　**17世紀**

Yomei Gate, Toshogu Shrine, 17th c.

48 桂離宮　書院　17世紀

Katsura Detached Palace, 17th c.

ていませんが、みなさんが京都へ行くと必ず案内される庭園があります。それは通称・苔寺、つまり西芳寺の庭園です。

　西芳寺の建物は瑠璃殿と呼ばれ、二層の華麗なものでしたが、火災でなくなり、数百年の間、放置されていたので、庭園の草木は茂り、湿気のために何百種という苔が自然に生えてしまいました。

　ところが今日、庭の廃墟に自然に生えたその苔の美しさによって、多くの人に愛されており、最も有名な寺院のひとつとなっています。庭園の骨格をなす自然の姿は壊されていないので、月日の経過につれて余計なものが取り去られ、むしろ苔によって真実の姿が表現されていると考えられているからです。この寺を創建したのは、日本庭園の祖といわれる夢窓国師（1275 〜 1351 年）でした。

▶「枯山水」　西芳寺の庭の中でも、**図版34**は石の庭園です。この庭石が、日本庭園にはひじょうに重要な意味を持っています。つまり、石は生きているもの、生命があるものと考え、「石を立てる」、あるいは「植える」という言い方をします。日本には、巨大な石に注連縄を張って、一つのサンクチュアリ（聖域）としてこれを礼拝する風習があります。

　その結果、木と水と石の庭園が、このように石ばかりの庭という形に凝縮されていきます。つまり、実際の池

during which the trees and grass of the former garden flourished wildly and moss grew in hundreds of varieties, aided by excessive dampness. As a result, this once-abandoned garden has now come to be widely appreciated for the uncommon beauty of its natural carpet of moss, and the "Moss Temple" ranks among the nation's most famous Buddhist sites.

Since the natural elements of the garden's original skeletal framework were not destroyed, the passage of time has rid the garden of extraneous flora and today it is the moss which is conceived to be the expression of religious truth. The temple was founded by Muso Soseki (1275-1351), "father" of the Japanese garden.

●注連縄を
張られた石

Rocks draped in shimenawa, a braided straw rope used for ritual purification. (Meoto-iwa "Wedded Rocks" at Futamigaura, Ise)

▶**Dry landscapes**　In Figure **34** we see Saihoji's rock garden. Rocks are especially important in Japanese gardens. Each rock is viewed to be a living object, and its placement in

49 金刀比羅宮　奥書院　上段の間　18世紀

Oku-shoin (Inner Drawing Room), Kotohiragu Shrine, 18th c.

や自然をさらにコンセントレートして、石と小さな砂によって、山と川を描くという方法が生まれるわけです。この庭の形式を、水を使わないので"枯山水"と呼びます。

▶**大仙院の庭**　図版35は、やはり京都の、大徳寺に所属する大仙院というお寺の小さな庭です。16世紀のはじめに造られたものですが、幅がほぼ3.4メートル、長さが5メートルほどしかありません。

しかし、ここでは中国の墨絵のように、岩は遠い山を表わし、白い砂は水をシンボライズしているといわれます。奥の方から川が流れ、手前には橋がかかっております。つまり1メートルほどの石を積み重ね、組み合わせることによって、巨大な自然の山や川、谷を走る激流を象徴しているわけで、単純、かつ微小なもので大きな自然、最も深い真実を表現したものとして、この庭園はひじょうに有名です。

中国のある詩人は、このような山の姿に仏の姿を見、川のせせらぎに釈迦の教えの声を聞いた、つまり自然の風景の中に仏教の真理を理解したという詩を書いております。このような小さな庭園が、いわゆる禅寺に造られているのは、そういう思想背景によります。

the garden is described as a "planting." Larger rocks are often roped off using a sacred Shinto festoon (*shimenawa*) and worshiped as a kind of sanctuary.

As a result, the term "garden," which usually implies trees and water and rocks, is reduced in scope to signify a garden of rocks alone. The pond and other elements of nature are still present but in concentrated form, with rocks and sand representing mountains and rivers. Since these gardens have no water, they are referred to as "dry landscapes" (*kare-sansui*).

▶ **The garden at Daisen-in** Figure **35** is a small but very famous garden at Daisen-in, which is part of Daitokuji Temple in Kyoto. Created in the beginning of the 16th century, the garden measures no more than about 5 meters in length and 2-3 meters in width, yet its large rocks are said to represent distant mountains and the white sand symbolizes water, much as in a Chinese ink painting.

The white water flows from the far end; a bridge lies across it in the foreground. This combination of rocks of only one meter or so in size creates the illusion of grandly imposing mountains and a fast-flowing river. It is a small, simple composition adeptly expressing nature, the deepest truth, but on grand scale.

A Chinese poet once wrote a verse describing how a natural vista such as this provided him with an understanding of the Buddhist truth. In the mountain he saw the outline of Buddha and in the murmuring brook he heard the voice of Buddha's teachings. It is from this conceptual background that small gardens like this came to be created at Zen temples.

50 遊楽図屏風　17世紀
"Merriments," 17th c.

51 洛中洛外図　上杉本　狩野永徳筆　16世紀

"Scenes In and Around Kyoto" (Uesugi version), by Kano Eitoku, 16th c.

▶**大名と城** このように簡素な寺院が建てられる一方で、16世紀から17世紀にかけて、諸国の大名たちは、競って華麗な城を築きました。その多くは19世紀の終わりの近代化の際に壊されたり、世界大戦で焼けてしまいましたが、最近、近代工法でいくつか再建されています。

図版**41**は松本城ですが、この城は創建当初のものがそのまま残された数少ないものの一つです。

一般に城というのは、石垣を築き、いくつかの層を建て、一の丸(まる)、二の丸、三の丸というブロックをつないでおります。ただ図版でごらんのように、ここでは実用性ではなく、きわめて装飾的な要素が強くなっています。屋根の繰り返しの美しさであるとか、天守閣、つまり最も高い建物と、突端にある魚の飾りなどに、その要素が見られます。

このような城が、城下町の中心にそびえ立ち、この中で侍たちは能や狂言を楽しんだわけであります。そして、この城を取り囲むようにしていくつかの寺院が設けられていました。

▶**能** 図版**38**はその当時、大名や武士たちが、戦陣の合間や城の中で好んだ能のマスクです。能の起源は、神の前で神に奉仕する儀礼的な演劇・神楽(かぐら)から始まり、それが娯楽的な猿楽(さるがく)として流行し、世阿弥(ぜあみ)(1363～1443年)によって、思想的に深められたドラマです。テーマ

▶**Feudal castles** While the early Japanese demonstrated a tendency toward plain, unadorned Buddhist temples such as those introduced here, around the 16th century the nation's feudal lords began to vie in constructing private castles of sumptuous splendor.

Unfortunately, almost all of these structures were razed toward the end of the 19th century as modernization set in, or went up in flames during World War II. But in recent years several have been reconstructed using modern construction methods.

Figure **41** is a picture of Matsumoto Castle, one of the few fortresses of its kind still extant in its original state.

As readily seen, feudal castles were monolithic structures fundamentally consisting of stone walls, multi-storied towers of varying height and several blocks of enclosures. But as the figure shows, the predominant factor in their construction does not seem to be practicality so much as decorative appeal.

Note, for example, the beauty of the redundant rooflines or the artistic flourish of the donjon topped by fish-like adornments pointed skyward. Castles of this ilk rose majestically at the focal point of their respective towns, and around their base Buddhist temples were established. Inside, the lords and their samurai, when they weren't fighting, took pleasure in viewing Noh drama and Kyogen farce.

▶**A Noh mask** Figure **38** shows a Noh mask. Noh's origins trace to the ritual dancing, or *kagura*, that was traditionally performed before the Shinto gods. Later it gained popularity as a form of entertainment known as *sarugaku* or "monkey music," and in the 14th century it was elevated to a serious dramatic art by Zeami (1363-1443).

52 婦女遊楽図屏風（松浦屏風）　17世紀
Genre scene, 17th c.

53 十二ヶ月風俗図　十一月「御火焚(おひたき)」　16世紀
"Ohitaki Festival" (November), one of a series of 12 genre paintings (calendar), 16th c.

は、神仙や高僧や妖怪や伝説など、きわめて多様ですが、極限状況における人間と、超越的なものとの交渉を描いたものが少なくありません。

能の面はきわめて単純な表情が、わずかな光線の変化、動作の変化によって、ひじょうに多くの表情を表現できるように工夫されております。**図版 39** は、その能を演じるステージ、つまり能舞台です。

▶**墨絵の三大特徴**　つづいて、当時の絵画に目を向けてみましょう。**図版 36** は、墨一色で描かれた雪舟（せっしゅう）（1420〜1506年）の風景画です。一般に日本の墨絵は、三つの点でヨーロッパの近代絵画とは異なっています。

一つはsignificant（シグニフィカント）、またはシンボル、つまり文学的な意味を求めるという点。二つ目はムーブメント、またはトレース、つまり筆を運んだ後、つまり手を動かした後を楽しむという点。三つ目はデコラティブ、つまり装飾性、デザイン性を重んじるという点です。つまり、単に風景を写すのではなく、風景の向こうにある自然と自分との一体感を描こうというもので、画面はその通過点に過ぎません。見る人は画面ではなく、画面を通過して自然の奥へ、自然との共感へと向かうわけです。

こういう発想は日常生活にもあります。人間関係でも、今もよく腹芸（はらげい）とか、悪い意味では腹を探るというような言い方をします。日本的交渉の悪い例として、国際的に悪評を買っていますが、これも、目に見える外側の

Thematically Noh embraces a broad range of subjects—everything from supernatural spirits and ghosts to high priests and legendary heroes. A frequent theme is interplay between man in extreme circumstances and these otherworldly beings. The Noh mask, despite its striking simplicity, is capable of conveying a full spectrum of emotions, each made possible by subtle changes in the use of lighting or movement. A Noh stage is shown in **Figure 39**.

▶**Japanese ink paintings** Next, let's look at the painting of the period. **Figure 36** is a monochrome landscape by the artist Sesshu (1420-1506). Broadly speaking, Japanese ink paintings differ from modern European artworks in three ways. First, in their portrayals of nature they seek to convey a certain significance either symbolic or literary. Second, they take pleasure in the final movement or traces of the brushwork. And third, they place emphasis on decorative demeanor or sense of artistic design.

The Japanese ink landscape therefore does not simply seek to recreate a scene realistically, but rather to describe the sense of communion with nature which extends beyond physical depiction.

In this sense, the canvas is no more than a corridor leading to a deeper truth. The viewer does not see the painting per se, but "passes through" the painting to the inner depths of nature, where he is able to discover a strong empathy with nature.

This same concept exists in everyday life. In their dealings with others the Japanese frequently refer to *haragei*, the "art of using one's stomach," or to *hara o saguru*, "probing someone's stomach." In both cases, the "stomach" symbolizes the gut center where a human being conceals his true sentiments, which may often diverge from apparent intentions

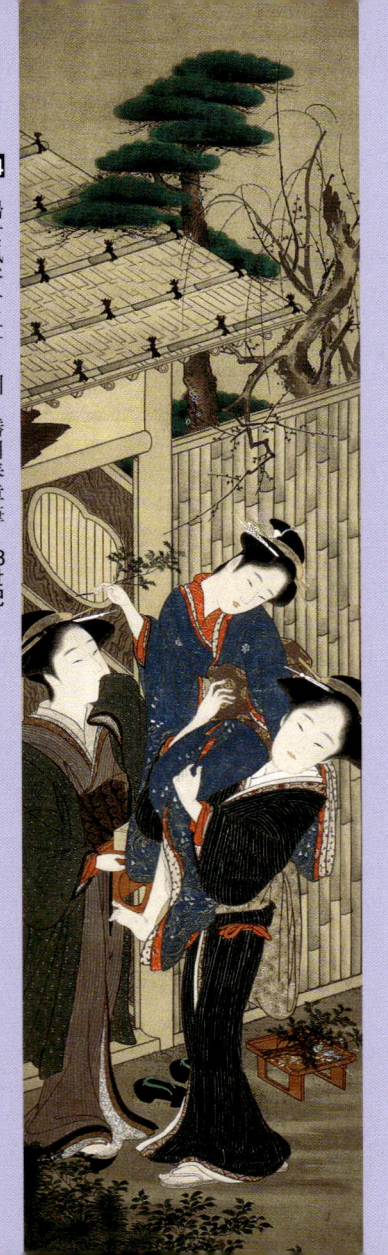

54 婦女風俗十二ヶ月図　勝川春章筆　18世紀
"Illustrations of the Twelve Months," by Katsukawa Shunsho, 18th c.

55 婦人相学十躰のうち浮気之相　喜多川歌麿筆　18世紀
"Coquettish Woman," by Kitagawa Utamaro, 18th c.

ものよりも、その奥に真実があるにちがいないという発想、真実は発言された言葉よりもその奥にあるはずだ、という考え方から来るものであります。

▶日本間の装飾美術　このような単純な墨絵が主として仏教寺院で描かれていたとき、有力な大名の城や皇族の邸では、対照的に華やかな襖絵が描かれました。図版40は狩野永徳（1543〜90年）の障壁画です。部屋の襖、つまり壁の仕切り戸に描かれています。つまり、美術を鑑賞するだけではなく、ある部屋やその場の雰囲気を作るという装飾的要素が強いということです。

　その最も代表的なものが、今も日本の畳の座敷に残っている"床の間"という装置です。この床の間は家の中心であり、そこに家の宝であるとか、その家の伝統をシンボライズするようなものを飾り、さまざまな儀式、パーティも床の間を中心に行なわれます。住居は住む道具ではなくて、むしろ一つのセレモニーのための装置として考えられています。

▶茶の湯と利休　図版42は最も有名な将軍・豊臣秀吉（1536〜98年）が、茶匠・利休に命じて作らせた、茶の湯に用いられる部屋、茶室です。ちょっと見ると、貧しい農家の小屋のようです。それが狙いだったのです。最高の富の所有者が、窮極に求めた形がこれでした。2畳台目といいまして、約1坪—3.3平米の広さしかあ

manifested through actions and words.

This ability of the Japanese to veil their real thoughts is often the butt of international criticism when it is sensed at bargaining tables or in similar situations.

But the Japanese know that more important than what is visible to the eye is the truth that lies within; truth rests deeper than words.

▶**Sliding panel decorations**　At about the same time that these simple monochrome ink paintings were being produced chiefly at Buddhist temples, richly colorful paintings were being favored as ornate decorations to *fusuma* sliding panels in feudal castles and aristocratic mansions. **Figure 40** shows one such painting by Kano Eitoku (1543-90).

Paintings of this genre, being applied directly to room partitions, were not merely intended to be enjoyed for their artistic beauty but also functioned as decorative accessories capable of creating a specific mood for a room or spatial zone.

The feature which perhaps plays the ultimate decorative role in Japanese architecture is the *tokonoma*, an alcove still found in most Japanese-style, i.e. *tatami*-matted, drawing rooms. The tokonoma serves as the symbolic center of the home and contains a family heirloom or other object which underscores the family's historic tradition. Many ceremonies and parties are also held with the tokonoma as focal point.

The Japanese home is thus viewed not as a box in which one lives but as a vessel in which ceremonies take place.

▶**The teahouse**　Figure **42** is a picture of a teahouse which Toyotomi Hideyoshi (1536-98), the most well-known of Japan's Shoguns, commissioned Sen no Rikyu (1522-91), the

りません。

　これをつくったのは、〈茶の湯〉を生活芸術として完成した天才・利休（1522〜91年）です。彼は最も派手好きな将軍であった秀吉に見出され、庇護されました。しかし、ついに最後は権力者の美意識と衝突して切腹させられたのです。利休はこのようなきわめて簡素な部屋も作っていますが、一方では黄金の茶室を作っています。このような二つの面がこの時代にはありました。

▶**茶室の室内空間**　この茶室は、なるたけ質素で単純なもののほうが、より自然に近く、人間の真実の姿が表現できる、という目的につらぬかれています。狭いから、より一層緊張した人間関係が生じるともいえます。

　私はここを訪ねて、この部屋にすわったことがありますが、天井はひじょうに低く、壁は、素材の泥や竹をそのまま出していて、空間は狭く、はじめは精神的な緊張を感じました。やがて緊張の限界を越えると、突然、自分が裸になったように感じられ、リラックスした気分が訪れ、やがて、茶室の壁を突きぬけて、自然のなかに気持ちが広がり、宇宙と溶けあうような一体感に喜びを感じていました。

　このような部屋で、最高権力者の将軍や、その周辺の人々が、茶をすすりながら、あるいは人生を振りかえり、あるいは重大な政治的・経済的決定をしたかと思うと、深い感慨に打たれます。

grand master of the tea ceremony, to build for him. As you see, the structure looks like a poor and simple shack. That was precisely the intention. It was a form of extreme humbleness sought by the nation's most wealthy individual. In all it has an area of only 3.3 meters, the size of two tatami mats.

The creator of this teahouse, Rikyu, was the genius who transformed the tea ceremony to a fine art intended to play an integral role in everyday life. Although he was initially taken under Hideyoshi's wing, he ultimately clashed with this most flamboyant of Japan's Shoguns over matters of artistic taste and was ordered by his benefactor to commit suicide. Besides extremely simple teahouses like the one which he created for Hideyoshi, Rikyu also designed sumptuous teahouses decorated in gold. This artistic duality is typical of the period.

▶**The teahouse interior** The teahouse pictured here was devised on the premise that the barer and simpler the structure, the closer it could approach nature and thus express the true meaning of humanity. Its cramped size was also seen to add a needed measure of tension to human relations.

I have personally visited this teahouse and sat inside it. At first I experienced a spiritual tension build within me, caused by the lowness of the ceiling, the mud and bamboo walls exposed to view, and the overall spatial restriction.

But once the limit of this tension had been surpassed, I suddenly felt naked, totally relaxed, my inner emotions expanding past the walls of the teahouse and beyond into nature, finally ending in the joy of feeling completely at one with the universe.

I was also deeply moved by the notion that it was precisely in the same room that Japan's most powerful Shogun and his

▶茶道具の芸術性　図版**45**は、その茶席で用いられた「水指し」、つまり水を入れる壺であります。茶の湯ではさらに花を生け、床に飾ることも行なわれました。その陶器の花生けも残されております。また何より大事な、茶を飲むための茶碗をはじめ、茶の湯に用いられる道具には、すべてさまざまな工夫が施されています。すべての茶道具は、最高の美術工芸品です。洗練の極致が追求されました。

　茶道と同時に、生花も華道として独立に完成しました。花を生けるということは、単なる花のデコレーションではありません。生けるとは、花の命を表現するという意味でした。もともとは仏の前に供えたものですが、自然の生命を尊重するという意味で、茶の湯の席でも欠くべからざるものとなりました。

▶茶席の花　茶席では、数多くの花を生けるようなことはしません。質素な部屋にふさわしいただ一輪の花、それも多くはまだ開ききらない蕾の状態で生けるのです。未だ完成していない状態のものを、無限の可能性が秘められているとして、尊いものと考えたからです。

　そして、その蕾に水を降りかけて、そのしずくを添えたまま生け、花が生きている状態を表わしたのです。まさに花一輪にも宇宙のドラマを演出したのです。

　茶の湯については、よく知られているように「わび」とか「さび」、あるいは最近では「渋み」という日本の

officers once sipped tea as they made major political or economic decisions or simply reflected on their lives.

▶ **Tea utensils**　All utensils used in the tea ceremony had to be artistic works of the highest standards, and the quintessence of refinement was at all times demanded. Figure **45** shows a *mizusashi,* a ceramic jar for holding water. Flower arranging and decoration in the tokonoma also formed an integral part of the tea ritual, and many ceramic vases of ancient origin exist from those days. Special designs were applied to all items used in the ceremony, including, of course, the tea bowls, which were of foremost importance.

Besides its role in the tea ceremony, flower arranging also came to be perfected as a separate discipline. To arrange flowers became more than just creating flower decorations.

As the word "ikebana" literally suggests, to *ikeru* or arrange flowers actually means to "give life" to them. Originally, flower arrangements were presented as offerings to Buddha, but later they became an indispensable element of the tea ceremony in view of the respect for natural life inherent in this ritual.

▶ **A single flower**　Rather than a bouquet, the tea ceremony calls for the arrangement of a single flower matching the plain, unpretentious atmosphere of the teahouse. In many cases, in fact, the flower is arranged while still in the bud, in appreciation of nature in its incomplete state, still imbued with limitless possibilities. Such a flower was arranged together with a sprinkling of water: the water droplets expressed the fact that the flower was alive. In this way, even a single flower played out the drama of the universe.

In describing the tea ceremony, the Japanese often use

美的姿勢が語られていますが、これは、物質的な貧しさの中でこそ真の心の豊かさを味わえるという態度を意味しています。また、人間の力で作り出したものよりも、自然そのものの力が感じられるものを大切にしたのです。

▶焼き物の魅力　先に紹介した**図版45**の陶器は割れています。でこぼこしていて、失敗作のように見えます。けっして滑(なめ)らかだとも、美しいとも考えられません。いきなりこういう壺を贈られたら、西欧の人々はどう感じるでしょうか。こんながらくたは困ると言って、怒るかもしれません。

　しかし、茶の湯の精神は、完成品よりも、この不完全さの中に自然の力をまざまざと見たわけです。

　焼き物というものは、人間の技術と計算を越えて、強い火から何かが生まれます。燃料の灰や煙が降りかかり、自然の釉薬(ゆうやく)となり、変化をつけます。窯(かま)の中の何千度という温度で生まれる偶然性、その偶然性の中に自然の力を発見し、その結果できたさまざまな変化こそが、焼き物の価値だと感じられたのです。

　焼き物の中には、自然のまさに創造の力が秘められているのです。

▶美しくない茶碗　**図版43**は茶の湯で用いられる茶碗です。志野(しの)焼のたいへん有名な作品で国宝ですが、形その

terms such as *wabi* and *sabi*—refined rusticity, subdued simplicity—and more recently *shibumi*, austere elegance. All of these concepts invoke the notion that true spiritual satisfaction can be attained only in a setting of materialistic humility. They also placed greater importance on the power of nature than on objects made by human hands.

This creative power of nature is most evident in pottery. The jar in **Figure 45**, for example, has cracks and an uneven surface. Lacking smoothness and beauty, it might lead you to conclude that the artist had failed and produced a highly flawed work. Indeed, if most Westerners received such a vase as a gift, they might pass it off as a piece of junk, or even become incensed at the giver. But in the tea ceremony, it is precisely in imperfection of this kind that the power of nature was recognized, for the creation of pottery extends beyond the technical skills and planning of man and is ultimately the work of the fire that seals its fate. Smoke and ashes rain down on each piece, producing natural glazes in endless variations. And in this unpredictability of the kiln, fired at temperatures reaching thousands of degrees, lies the power of nature. The value of each finished piece is set according to factors that remain beyond the control of the potter.

▶ **A National Treasure tea bowl**   In **Figure 43** we see a tea bowl of the kind used in the tea ceremony. It is a highly well-known piece in the Shino style and has been designated a National Treasure, yet it too is irregular in shape and by no means "beautiful" in the conventional sense. It contrasts sharply with the flawlessly regular, geometrically proportioned white and celadon porcelain vases that were imported from China and Korea and were favored for the tea ceremony in its embryonic stage. Gradually, however, Japanese tastes took

ものは歪(ゆが)んでいて、けっして美しくはありません。中国や韓国から輸入された白磁(はくじ)や青磁(せいじ)の壺は、たいへん幾何(きか)学的に整った美しいものです。

　実は茶の湯でもはじめのうちは、整った陶器を用いていました。ところが、日本人の好みにしたがい、しだいにこのような不完全な形のものが好まれてゆきました。それを決定的な美学にしたのが利休です。

　茶の湯を完成した利休は、特に土物(つちもの)と言われ、低い温度で焼かれる日本の陶器をひじょうに愛しました。しかも轆轤(ろくろ)を用いないで、手で形を作ります。この不完全の中に、人間と自然との共同作業が味わわれるからです。事実、これを手に取ってみますと、手のひらの中にしっくりと落ちついて、なじんで感じられて、温かくヒューマンな感じがするのは不思議です。

▶戦国武将の美的生活　図版**44**の一見汚れた黒い茶碗はその代表作例です。黒一色で低い温度で作られ、温かい感じがします。この焼き物を作った窯元(かまもと)の家は、今でも続いて、京都で楽焼(らくやき)を作っています。

　いうまでもなく、これらは国宝、ないしはそれに準じるもので、価格はつけられないほどですが、たとえ数億円をもってしても買うことはできません。事実、戦国時代の武将の一人は、国一国、領地の代わりに、茶碗の名品一つを所望(しょもう)して断わられたという歴史的挿話(そうわ)も残されているくらいです。あの荒々しい戦国武将の時代に、こ

precedence and irregular, imperfect ceramic pieces came to be preferred. This "preference" was eventually transformed to a definitive aesthetic by Rikyu.

Rikyu especially valued an earthy variety of Japanese pottery fired at low temperature and shaped completely by hand, without the assistance of a potter's wheel. He appreciated this imperfect style because it exemplified a collaborative effort between man and nature. If you could take a tea bowl of this kind and hold it in your hand, you would discover that it fits quite comfortably and naturally, with almost a "human" quality about it.

▶**An episode of a warrior general** The "tarnished-looking" black bowl shown in Figure **44** is a prime example. Fired at low temperature, it is entirely black and projects an aura of pleasing warmth. The kiln where it was produced is still in operation in Kyoto, dedicated to the production of Raku ware, a soft, low-fired, lead-glazed ceramic primarily used in the tea ceremony.

Needless to say, the various pottery pieces discussed here, all being National Treasures or equivalent works, are without price and could not be purchased even for millions of yen. There is even an anecdote in the annals of Japanese history that tells of a certain warlord of the Warring States period (15-16th centuries) who once proposed—unsuccessfully, alas—to exchange his entire fiefdom for a single tea bowl of great renown. Little would one expect, during a time of fierce and incessant battling, to hear of a warrior general so intent on pursuing a life centered on aesthetics.

のような美的生活を追求していたということも驚くべきことです。

4. 近世の世界（江戸時代）

▶日光・東照宮　さて、江戸時代の代表的建築を二点見てみましょう。まず**図版 47** は、およそ300年ほど前、1645年に建てられた日光の東照宮（とうしょうぐう）です。これは江戸幕府を創った徳川家康（1542～1616年）の墓で、彼は神の化身として祭られました。この建物は、ごらんのように大変デコラティブで、またエネルギッシュです。

先に、古代日本文化における縄文（じょうもん）的なものと弥生（やよい）的なもの、荒々しいものと静かなものという二つの要素について述べましたが、東照宮はたいへんエネルギッシュで、派手で縄文的な作品の代表といえるでしょう。人工の装飾の限りを尽くして、今まで見た茶の湯の美とはまったく違って見えます。

しかもこのデコレーションには、中国のエピソードを彫刻として彫り込んだものもありますし、オランダからの灯籠（とうろう）もここにあります。きわめて国際的な文化を取り入れています。

しかし、ドイツの建築家のブルーノ・タウトという人は、これを見て、いかにも成金（なりきん）趣味で、悪趣味であると非難しました。彼はこの建物だけを自然から切り離して考えたのですが、実はこの建物は標高1800メートルの山の麓（ふもと）に、山を切りひらいて建てられているのです。

4. The Modern Period (Edo)

▶**Toshogu Shrine** Now let's look at two representative examples of Edo-period architecture. The first is Toshogu Shrine at Nikko, built more than three centuries ago in 1645 (Figure **59**). It was constructed as the mausoleum of Tokugawa Ieyasu (1542-1616), the founder of the Tokugawa Shogunate in Edo who came to be deified as an incarnation of the gods. As you see, the building is highly decorative and "energetic."

Earlier I spoke of the two principal elements of ancient Japanese culture—the dynamic, aggressive Jomon influence and the peaceful, quiescent Yayoi influence. In Toshogu we recognize the more flamboyant, Jomon aspect.

The shrine not only takes artificial decoration to its very limits but also embodies a type of beauty completely different from what we saw in the tea ceremony. Its decorative features are also remarkably international in scope, and include carvings that depict episodes from Chinese lore, and lanterns from Holland.

The German architect Bruno Taut (1884-1938) once criticized it as gaudy and vulgar. His condemnation, however, was based on an evaluation of Toshogu as a structure independent of its natural surroundings. Toshogu stands at a height of 1,800 meters in a beautiful valley carved out of a mountain named Mt. Nantai. Midway up the mountain is a crystalline lake called Chuzenji, and in early days the entire mountain including the lake was worshiped as a divine power.

Toshogu was placed at the very center of this holy setting, in the womb of nature so to speak, and it therefore acts, in concentrated scope, as a symbol of its overall surroundings. In this respect, it represents the supreme fusion of Buddhist

その山は男体山(なんたいさん)といい、かつて神として崇拝されていました。

山の中腹には中禅寺湖(ちゅうぜんじこ)という湖があり、山と湖を含んだ巨大な地域自体が、神として信仰されていたのです。東照宮は、その地域全体の中心に置かれたもので、いわば、自然の胎内にコンセントレート（凝集(ぎょうしゅう)）された信仰の姿を見ることができます。仏教建築が、日本の山岳信仰と結合した最高の結晶といえます。

▶**桂離宮**　このようなきわめて装飾的な将軍の廟(びょう)を祭る建物とほぼ同じ時期に、ときの天皇の兄弟である貴族（八条宮智仁親王(はちじょうのみやとしひとしんのう)）が、京都の桂川(かつらがわ)のほとりに、別荘を造りました。桂離宮(かつらりきゅう)です（**図版48**）。

これを見ますと、最初に紹介した伊勢神宮（**図版10**）であるとか、京都御所（**図版20**）につながる伝統が引き継がれています。木の皮で葺(ふ)いた屋根、単純な柱のデザイン、高い床(ゆか)、三つのブロックに分かれ、長い廊下でつながっている建物、長く差し出た庇(ひさし)、きわめて低い平面的な配置など、機能と単純さが緊張した美しさを表わしています。

現代の建築家は、きわめて合理的なシステムから成っていると感嘆しています。とくに、白い障子(しょうじ)と柱との比例は黄金分割にひとしく、またモンドリアンなどの、現代絵画の美しさに通じると評する人もいます。つまり、20世紀に入ってからの世界の美術の原型が、ここ

architecture and mountain worship.

▶**Katsura Detached Palace**　At about the same time that this extremely ornate mausoleum was being built at Nikko to enshrine a Shogun, off in Kyoto on the bank of the Katsura River a villa was under construction by Prince Toshihito (1579-1629) of the Hachijo no Miya family, brother of reigning Emperor Goyozei. This is the Katsura Detached Palace (Figure **48**).

As we see, the structure draws on the architectural tradition of the Ise Shrine (Figure **10**) and Kyoto Imperial Palace (Figure **20**) which we examined earlier: the bark-thatched roof, the simple design of the pillars, the raised floors, the division into three separate blocks, buildings connected by long corridors, the broadly overhanging eaves, the generally low profile of the structures.

The palace is an expression of intense beauty combining functionalism and simplicity. Even today, modern architects marvel at its rational and systematic design, especially the exquisite proportionalism of its white *shoji* screens and pillars, which corresponds precisely to the golden section. Some have even likened the palace's beauty to a modern Neo-Plasticist painting by Mondrian. In the Katsura Detached Palace, such critics say, we can therefore see a prototype of 20th-century art.

に見られるというのです。

▶**桂離宮の庭園**　桂離宮では、建物とともに庭園が重要です。むしろ建物は、池のある庭を取り巻くように配置されています。この庭園と質素な亭(あずまや)で茶の湯を楽しみ、また華やかな歌舞音曲の集まりを催し、春は花見、秋は紅葉(もみじ)狩りと、王朝さながらの光景でした。

池に舟を浮かべて和歌、俳諧(はいかい)を作るという、セレモニーやパーティも行なわれたことでしょう。今も、この庭園を歩いてゆくと、私たちは、単なる建物と庭ではなく、一つの完結した世界に入り、真の自然の姿を味わうことを教えられるのです。

このように、川のほとりに、自然と調和して造られた建物が一方にはあり、また同じ時代に、日光東照宮が自然と対峙(たいじ)して山に造られました。しかもこの対照的な二つの建築物が、同じ大工の棟梁(とうりょう)によって造られているということは、まさに驚くべきことです。日本古代からの二つの対立的要素が見事に現われた例と言えます。

さらに江戸時代の大きな特徴は、将軍や天皇を取り巻く貴族のほかに、市民の生活が文化に浮かび上がってきたことです。ようやく風景や建物ばかりではなく、市民の日常生活が、文学、美術、建築に採(と)りあげられるようになります。

▶**The garden of Katsura**　As I have already pointed out, at the Katsura Detached Palace, as elsewhere, the garden plays as important a role as the buildings. In fact, we might describe the setting as a number of structures built around a central garden with a large pond.

Here, the aristocrats of the day would gather for ceremonies or parties just as at the Imperial Palace. In the rustically simple arbor they would partake of a tea ceremony or a festive performance of music and dance. On the pond they would set out in boats to compose poetry or haiku. In spring they would view the cherry blossoms; in autumn they would collect the fallen maple leaves.

Even today, when we walk through this garden we see more than just a garden and buildings; we are drawn into a complete world—a world where we can view nature in microcosm.

From the same period we have a villa constructed on the bank of a river in harmony with its natural surroundings and a shrine erected on a mountain surrounded by nature. What is perhaps even more surprising than the contemporaneity of these two architectural masterpieces, however, is the fact that they were built by the same master carpenter. His contrasting creations brilliantly illustrate the dual elements of Japanese culture passed down from ancient times.

▶**Popular society**　Besides the cultural heritages of the Shogunate and of the aristocracy surrounding the Emperor, a third fundamental aspect of the Edo period is the emergence of a popular culture based on the lives of ordinary citizens. Gradually, cultural influences extended beyond their earlier limits of architecture and natural scenery, and the lives of ordinary people came to be taken up in the literature, art and architecture of the period.

▶市民の姿と生活　絵画の分野では、このころから、京都に住む庶民の四季折々の生活を描いた「洛中洛外図」という屏風絵が、盛んに描かれています。中でも図版**51**は、最も有名な作品です。

　このように庶民、または市民の生活が描かれるということは、ヨーロッパでは19世紀の後半になってからですから、日本で16、17世紀にすでに市民生活が描かれているという事実は、江戸時代の社会が、市民経済的にも成熟していたことを示していると言えるでしょう。

　図版 **7** では、獅子のお面をかぶった人が踊っています。これは悪魔をはらう正月の宗教的儀式です。この獅子舞はつい最近まで正月に日本で行なわれていました。今でも田舎では行なわれています。

▶遊女の風俗と生活　ところで、江戸の華はなんと言っても遊女でした。遊女は本質的にはプロスティチュート（娼婦）ですが、高級な遊女は、客の選択権と拒否権を持っていました。彼女らは廓という特殊な地域に生活を限定されましたが、その中では、むしろハイクラスの社交界を形成していたのです。歌舞伎の中でも、吉原の踊りや、「三人吉三廓初買」などに、遊女の風俗が数多く採りあげられています。

　それは、彼女らは最高の身分の客を相手とするため、詩歌、管絃、踊りなどの高い教養を身につけるよう、幼い頃から教育されていたからです。また、封建身分社会

Even before the Edo period, during the 16th century numerous paintings were created on folding screens which portrayed everyday life in and around Kyoto. One of the most famous works of this genre is shown in **Figure 51**. The adoption of everyday life as an artistic theme did not take place in Europe until the second half of the 19th century. But as we have seen, in Japan such works were already flourishing as early as the 16th and 17th centuries. This reflects the maturation of Japanese popular society, especially in economic terms, during the Edo years.

In **Figure 7** we see men dancing in the guise of a lion. This is a religious ritual being performed at a new year celebration to exorcise evil spirits. Lion dances like this were performed regularly at the beginning of a new year in Japan until quite recently, and even today they continue in various outlying areas.

▶ **The demimonde** One of the central protagonists of Edo society were the courtesans of the demimonde. Essentially prostitutes by profession, courtesans of higher status actually had the right to select or refuse a client. Though they lived in special "red-light" districts, within these segregated precincts unfolded an elaborate world of high society. Kabuki plays, for example, often treat themes pertaining to the manners and customs of these ladies of charm, including dancing and other skills.

Since their vocation was to entertain clients of high social standing, courtesans were educated from an early age in the finer arts such as poetry, music and dance. Paradoxically, it was also only within the confines of the Edo demimonde that members of the rigid feudal society were accorded the freedom to engage in genuine exchanges of love and passion.

にあっては、廓だけが、逆説的に純粋な恋愛や情熱の許される場所でした。

　ごらんのように、**図版 50**、**52** では遊里における市民生活が描かれています。ここで描かれた着物の柄は、たいへん美しく派手ですが、絵のために特別に描かれたものではなく、実際に用いられたものです。同じような衣裳が今日でも残っていて、博物館へ行くと見ることができます。

▶**肉筆浮世絵**　**図版 54** の女性の姿は、肉筆で描かれたものですが、これをさらに版木に彫って刷ったものが「浮世絵」です。この図においても、クローズ・アップし、デフォルメされた単純な線の美しさ、力強さ、また全体の姿の動きをはらんだダイナミズム、それから表情や肩のやさしい女らしさ、わずかにのぞいている足の指のエロティシズム、それらすべてが洗練された女性の美しさを表現しています。

▶**歌麿の女性表現**　**図版 55** は最も有名な浮世絵師、歌麿が十種類の女性を描いた作品の一つです。歌麿は女性をよく観察して、その性格を描き分けました。この女は「浮気の相」と題されています。ひじょうにふくよかな洗練された線が、顔から肩、胸、それから指などにみずみずしい女性の魅力を表現しています。

　絵画としてみると、線が単純化されています。しか

Figures 50 and 52 depict the everyday lives of these denizens of the gay quarters. Their kimonos, as we see, are extremely beautiful if somewhat immodest. They were not drawn this way simply for the purposes of art but are authentic representations of actual garb, some of which has survived through the centuries and is on view in museums.

▶ **Ukiyoe** Figure 54 is a brushdrawn painting of three women. During the Edo period, paintings such as these were frequently carved in wood from which hand-rubbed prints were made—prints renowned throughout the world as "ukiyoe." Here we see the subjects in close-up, their beauty described through simple, suggestive lines. We recognize a certain strength, as well as dynamism of movement. And we detect femininity in their expression and the lines of their shoulders, and eroticism in the faintly visible toes. Together these elements express the ideal of refined, feminine beauty of the period.

▶ **A portrait by Utamaro** Figure 55 shows a female portrait by the most famous of all ukiyoe artists, Utamaro (1753-1806). It is one of a well-known series of ten woodblock prints all depicting women in different poses. Utamaro was a true master at observing and capturing the traits and personalities of his subjects.

The woman shown here, for example, represents the theme of romantic infidelity. The voluptuous, refined lines of her face and shoulders, her bosom, even her fingers, all express the sensuous attractiveness of a tender young woman. Though the artistic strokes themselves are somewhat simplistic, with a mysterious power they convey the essence of feminine emotions, creating an ideal of femininity that we can still

し、ひじょうに洗練された線は、充分に女性らしい情感を表わしており、理想的な女性像として今日でも充分に通じるものです。

　ご存じのように、浮世絵は、19世紀にフランス印象派の画家たちに大きな影響を与えました。その理由は、雪舟の絵（**図版36**）を紹介したときにも述べたとおり、ここでも第一に単純な線による文学性、第二に象徴的な表現、第三に装飾性という三つの要素を挙げることができます。

▶**真の女性美**　このように日本人の生活は、きわめて美的な態度につらぬかれていると言っても差しつかえありません。その美しさの根底には、自然との交流があります。したがって、浮世絵などには、ひじょうにエロティックなものはありますけれども、女性の全裸ヌードが描かれることは、あまりありません。

　隠されている方が、より一層その奥にある魅力を強く表現することができると信じているからです。『源氏物語』は、ひじょうに数多くの男女の愛情、それから肉体関係を細かく描いていますが、いわゆるベッドシーンを描写していません。それは、目に見える現実よりも、隠されたところに真実がある、真の女性の魅力は、やはり隠されたところにあると考えられていたからにほかなりません。

relate to today.

As is well known, Japan's ukiyoe art form was to exert a great influence on the French Impressionists of the 19th century. These effects were seen in the same three areas I spoke of in introducing Sesshu's painting earlier (**Figure 36**): literary appeal based on linear simplicity, symbolistic expression and decorative quality.

▶**The ideals of feminine beauty**   From what we have seen so far we can now state, without exaggeration, that the everyday lives of the Japanese are indeed interwoven with an extremely artistic thread. At the foundation of this artistic beauty is the communion between man and nature. Accordingly, though we do find certain erotic themes in ukiyoe, we only rarely come across depictions of the nude female body. This is because the artist believed that there is a stronger, deeper erotic appeal in the art of suggestive concealment.

The Tale of Genji too speaks of the love affairs and physical relations of numerous men and women, yet there are no carnal scenes ever described. Truth, the Japanese believed, lay in what was left hidden rather than what was open to view, and this philosophy unquestionably applied to ideals of feminine beauty as well.

Ⅳ. 結び──現代に生きる〈茶の湯〉の精神

▶**伝統芸術の結合**　最初に「雪月花」について論じ、次に詩や俳句を紹介し、さらには建築、絵画、陶器などを採りあげてきましたが、最も大事なことは、それらがそれぞれの芸術ジャンルの範囲内に留（とど）まるものではなく、一つの生き方として、総合的に製作・享受（きょうじゅ）されていることです。よく例に挙げられますが、茶の湯はその典型です。いわば、茶の湯は伝統的芸術の複合体です。

たとえば、茶の湯自体は、利休自身が述べていることですが、「湯を沸（わ）かし、お茶を茶碗で飲む」という行為に尽きるわけです。ところが、そのセレモニーの支度（したく）は、それよりずっと以前から始まります。これは、自然を主人公とした一種の宗教劇だと言ってもいいくらいです。

まず亭主は、どういう人間を組み合わせるか、また、どのような道具を組み合わせて、ドラマを表現するかを考え、知恵をしぼります。これは〈取合（とりあ）わせ〉と呼ばれ、古くは、平安宮廷の〈歌合わせ〉〈貝合わせ〉〈もの合わせ〉などという遊び方の流れを汲（く）むもので、多くは、詩歌や物語の文学的主題にしたがって組み立てられます。

招待状が発送され、客として呼ばれた人は、これらの象徴からテーマを理解し、推理し、主人の用意した意図

IV. CONCLUSION
——The Tea Ceremony Spirit in Modern Japan

▶ **A composite of traditional arts**　In this presentation I set out by discussing the cultural innuendoes of "snow, moon and flowers," followed by an introduction to Japan's principal poetic forms, waka and haiku, and finally a random look at Japanese architecture, painting and pottery.

In review, it should be noted that each of these aspects of Japanese culture, dealt with separately here, is in fact not confined to the scope of its particular artistic genre but is part of a comprehensive legacy that passes from generation to generation as a way of life.

The tea ceremony is a good example. In it we find a composite of traditional arts. The ceremony itself might be likened to a religious play in which nature plays the leading role.

In one sense, as Rikyu himself remarked, the tea ceremony is nothing more than the boiling of water and the act of drinking tea. Upon analysis, however, we see that there is a great deal of preparation involved before the ceremony.

First, the host must compile his guest list, always keeping in mind the mutual relations of his guests. Next he must determine what kind of artistic drama to act out, based on the implements which he selects to use.

Gatherings of this kind are a cultural offshoot of entertainments enjoyed at the Heian court, games in which poems or objects were compared for amusement. With the tea ceremony, the host plans for the events to proceed according to a theme drawn from poetry or literature.

He inserts clues of his intention into his invitations, and the

を汲みとることが求められています。つまり、茶会は文学的テーマにしたがったドラマです。

▶茶室への招待　さて当日、招かれた客は、まず門から待合（まちあい）へ、そして庭園に入ります。茶の湯の会合では、この入り口から茶室に至るプロセスもきわめて重要です。道は露路（ろじ）といいますが、庭園から茶室へと続く小道には、石が飛び飛びに埋められています。客は、その石を踏み、導かれて、茂った木立（こだち）の間を縫って行くわけです。そうする間に、茶室に入る心の準備をします。

　視界に、しだいに姿を表わしてくる茶室は、質素で樹木の中に埋もれ、まるで自然の一部としか見えません。ときには掃除をした後で、露路（ろじ）にわざわざ枯れた松葉を散らして、より自然らしくすることもあります。

　茶室の横には、身を清めるために手を洗い、口をそそぐ水をたたえた、蹲（つくばい）という石が置いてあります。蹲には、竹の筒の筧（かけい）で近くの清流から引かれたひとすじの水がしたたっています。

　時に、鹿などを追い払うために山の家で工夫している竹筒の装置の模倣（もほう）を作り、竹筒が石に当たって発するカーンという響きで、自然の浄寂（じょうじゃく）をいっそう深く味わったりもします。

▶茶室への入室　このようなプロセスを通した後に部屋に入るのですが、それも小さな入り口から身をかがめて

guests are expected to recognize the theme from the symbols provided. In this respect, the tea ceremony is like a drama founded on a literary theme.

▶ **The path to the teahouse** The procedure for entering the teahouse is of extremely great importance. Just before the appointed time the guests enter through the gate, proceed first to a small waiting area and then to the garden proper.

A narrow path paved with flagstones then leads through the garden toward the teahouse, weaving the guests slowly through a well-tended grove of shrubbery and trees. This draws them into the appropriate mood of solemnity for the ceremony which is to follow.

Gradually the teahouse, humble and simple, comes into view through the foliage and undergrowth, almost giving the impression that it, like everything else in sight, is a work of nature. At times the host heightens the overall effect by deliberately scattering withered pine leaves through the garden after he has swept it clean.

The guests continue as far as the *tsukubai*, an arrangement of stones to one side of the teahouse comprising a basin of clear water where they symbolically purify themselves by rinsing the hands and mouth. The water is drawn from a clear stream over a bamboo conduit, creating a thin ribbon of water.

In some cases, a deer chaser is improvised whereby the water gradually fills a bamboo tube until it dashes against the stone, as if to scare away nearby animals. The reverberation of the bamboo hitting the stone makes the ensuing silence of nature all the more impressive.

忍び込まなければなりません。すると、室内からお香のにおいがただよってきます。

　多くの場合、床(とこ)の間の壁には、高僧が禅の悟りの境地を書き表わした書＝墨蹟(ぼくせき)が飾られ、床には一本の花が生(い)けてあります。ここではじめて客と亭主が相対(あいたい)して、一服の茶を点(た)て、飲むのです。お茶を飲む行為それ自体よりも、それまでのプロセスがいかに重要かがわかります。

▶「一期一会(いちごいちえ)」　茶の湯の心を最もよく表現したと言われているのは「一期一会」というフレーズです。この語の意味するところは、たとえいつも出会う友人であっても、この茶席での出会いは一生にただ一度の機会だ、今日が最後の機会だ、だから全力を尽(つ)くして永遠に変わらぬ心情を通わさなければならないということです。

　一人と一人が、永遠に変わることなく深い心を交(か)わすということは、何によって支えられるのでしょうか。友情だけでは足りません。人間は不安定で、弱いものだからです。そこで、人は自然との一体感を互いに共有することによって、友情もまた支えられると考えました。それによって、自分の今日の人生そのものを、永遠の生命として完成させようと心がけるのです。

　ここには、天台宗から禅に流れる「久遠即今日(くおんこんにち)」、すなわち〈Eternal now〉という概念が主張されています。茶の湯の家元、利休の子孫は、この now、すなわち今日(こんにち)

▶ **Entering the teahouse**   Only after these procedures have been completed are the guests ready to enter the teahouse. To do so, they must crouch low and crawl through a tiny entrance. Inside the teahouse, the scent of incense fills the room.

In the tokonoma there is often a calligraphy scroll by a high priest describing the state of Zen enlightenment, complemented by a single flower in a vase. It is at this time, finally, that the host appears to greet his guests and begins preparing the tea. From this it can be easily understood that the process leading up to the tea ceremony is actually more important than the drinking of the tea itself.

▶ **The phrase "ichigo-ichie"**   The underlying philosophy of the tea ceremony is perhaps best described with the phrase *ichigo-ichie*, literally "one life, one meeting."

What this means is that each encounter with someone, even a friend whom you see often, should be treated as if it were a once-in-a-lifetime occurrence—as if today were the last time you might meet. Based on this recognition, you should feel strongly committed to make every effort, through selfless solicitude, to strengthen the bonds of eternal friendship between yourself and the other person.

What enables two persons to feel so deeply, so eternally, for each other? Friendship alone is not enough, for man is a weak and unstable being. Instead, friendship must be supported by a commonly shared sense of oneness with nature, a feeling that elevates man's fleeting, earthly existence to the changeless realm of eternity. This is the role of the tea ceremony—to provide the setting for this emotional transformation.

As a philosophy, this pursuit of the "eternal now" originated in the Tendai sect and passed on into Zen. Even today descendants of Rikyu, founder of the tea ceremony, use the

を名として、今日庵(こんにちあん)と名のっています。

▶**柔道と柔術の違い**　日本では、生(い)け花、茶の湯、書などに「道」という語をつけて、茶道、華道、書道などと呼びます。よく知られている柔道の「道」も同じです。柔術と言うときは、技術―テクニックに重点を置いていますが、「道」がつくと、単なる技術ではなく、人生の歩んでいく道、一生涯を意味します。つまり、柔道という場合は、人生の生き方、精神的な目標を意味するわけです。

　つまり、道はたんに歩く道路ではなく、絶対的な真理、または、そこへいたるプロセスを意味しています。目的と過程が同じというのは矛盾して聞こえますが、過程の一瞬一瞬に、すでに完成された真実が現われるというのが、〈Eternal now〉という考え方です。

▶**東洋の死生観**　その人生の道行きの先にあるのは何か。それは、言うまでもなく死であります。現代は少しでも長く生きること、死を人生から追い払うことに全力を尽くしています。しかし、本来、東洋や日本では、人はその人生において、つねに死へ向かって自分をより美しく完成させることに努めなければならないと考えました。つねに美的な生き方を通して、自然に戻ることを目指したわけです。少なくとも、そこに最も理想的な生き方が表わされていると言うことができるでしょう。

word "now" (*konnichi*) as part of their professional title.

▶ **A never-ending goal** The tea ceremony and other disciplines discussed in the preceding pages—flower arranging, calligraphy and so on—are each referred to in Japanese using words including the suffix *do* literally meaning "path" and often translated as "The Way": *sado*, "The Way of Tea," *kado*, "The Way of Flowers," *shodo*, "The Way of Calligraphy," etc.

The same suffix is found in the term "judo," where the addition of *do* signifies that the undertaking is intended to serve as a "path" or "way" of life—a never-ending goal. The term is distinguished from "jujitsu," which emphasizes the technical aspects of this sport rather than its spiritual discipline. In all cases, *do* is more than a path; it is an absolute truth, as well as the process leading toward that truth. It may sound contradictory for a goal and the process leading toward it to be identical. But according to the philosophy of "eternal now" each moment along the way in itself is a completed truth.

▶ **The ideal way of life** What destiny then lies at the end of every path in life? Inevitably, death. Today the goal of mankind is to extend life as long as possible, to do everything in one's power to keep death from his doorstep.

In earlier times, however, in the Orient, and particularly in Japan, the goal in life was to strive for personal improvement, to aim for spiritual beauty or perfection throughout life as one marched inevitably toward death. Through this attainment of inner beauty man sought to return to nature. This, at least, was seen to be the ideal way of life on earth.

Why is such high value placed on nature? To quote from

どうして自然に価値があるのでしょうか。仏の教えに〈山川草木悉有仏性〉という言葉があります。自然の山も川も草も木も人間も動物も、生物も無生物も、すべてある巨大で統一的な真理の現われの一様相にすぎないということです。

そこに日本人は神を見ました。仏の悟りと神とは重なり、同じ位を持つようになり、自然の法則には人間以上の絶対的真理がある、自然に従うことが、永遠の叡智——ハンニャハラミタ——にいたることであり、そこでは至福が約束されていると考えたのです。

▶日本人の倫理性　先年、外国の方にこのような話をしたところ、次のような質問を受けました。日本人の生活態度は確かに美的かもしれない。しかし、その倫理性というものは、どこにあるのか、その基準はどこにあるのか、というきわめて厳しいものでした。

これはおそらく外国人が日本人とさまざまな交渉を持つときに、日本人には、たとえばキリスト教やイスラム教における戒律のような倫理的基準がないということからくる戸惑いかもしれません。私も実のところたいへん困りました。

確かに日本人にとっても倫理的ということはひじょうに重要ですが、キリスト教やユダヤ教のような戒律は日常生活にはありません。むしろ戒律を好みません。インドやビルマ、中国、チベットに残されている仏教は、日

Buddhist teachings, "The spirit of Buddha is found in all mountains, rivers, grasses and trees." All objects of nature, animate and inanimate—mountains, rivers, grasses, trees, human beings, animals—are manifestations of a great universal truth, and all contain absolute truth within them.

The earliest Japanese viewed these truths as deities. Later, these gods came to overlap with Buddhist enlightenment on an equal plane, and the laws of nature held an absolute truth above the laws of mankind. Acting in accordance with the ways of nature was the path toward eternal wisdom, known in Sanskrit as *prajñā pāramitā*, where supreme happiness is to be found.

▶**Japanese morality** Last year when I gave a talk similar to this to a foreign audience, someone posed the following question: "Granted, as you've said, that the Japanese attitude toward life may be oriented toward the aesthetic. But where is Japanese morality to be found, and on what concepts is it based?"

This is a very imposing question, one which may arise from the suspicion, during various negotiations between foreigners and Japanese, that the Japanese lack the same kind of moral standards that are part and parcel, for example, of Christianity or Islam. To be quite truthful, I was at a loss how to answer.

Although, without question, morality is an extremely important consideration even for the Japanese, unlike Christianity or Judaism there are no religious commandments governing everyday life.

On the contrary, such precepts are anathema. The prevailing form of Buddhism still found in India, Burma, China and Tibet is Hīnayāna (Theravada), the so-called "Lesser Vehicle" that places great weight on rules for everyday living.

常的な戒律を重んじる小乗仏教が大部分です。

　しかし日本では、とても守れない表面だけの戒律は現実的でないと考えました。そして出家した僧侶ばかりでなく、一般人も守れる戒律はないかと考え、いわば自然の法則というものに到達しました。そこに、古代から神道として身につけていた宗教倫理的な感覚が一致しました。日本では大乗仏教、つまり、大衆的な仏教が支配的です。

　日本の神道のおそらく唯一の戒律は、穢れをきらうことです。穢れは、たんに物質的清潔さばかりではなく、心の清潔・クリーンを意味しています。それが美的倫理に見えるのです。

▶「潔い」ということ　ここまで述べてきたような歴史的な日本人の生き方、考え方を振り返り、また私や私の友人などの生き方というものを同時に反省してみますと、やはり倫理性というのは、一種のこの美的な態度に貫かれていると思います。

　武士は死ぬときに「潔い」ということを最も大事な規範としました。「潔い」というのは、やはり倫理的な穢れを取り除き、美的に死を迎える態度ということになるでしょうか。しかし、その美的ということは西洋の人工的な美ではなくて、自然との一致、自然との共感を損なわないということに重点を置いているのです。

　それを一言で言いますと、最初に述べました「雪月

In Japan, such rules were deemed impractical, superficial and too demanding to obey to the letter.

In their place the Japanese sought a set of rules that could be readily followed not just by devout monks but even by the layman, whereupon they hit on the laws of nature. Obeyance of natural laws was a concept that coincided harmoniously with the religious ethic that was already ingrained in the Japanese through their centuries-old belief in Shinto.

As a result, the Japanese embraced Mahāyāna Buddhism, the "Greater Vehicle" which was more in keeping with the needs of the popular masses.

There is, I would suggest, one commandment inherent in Japanese Shinto: the injunction against defilement. Defilement relates here not merely to physical cleanliness but to "cleanliness" of the heart. This commandment is seen in Japan's aesthetic ethic.

▶**The foremost criterion**　In reply, I would like to refer again to the lifestyles and philosophies the Japanese have embraced throughout their history, as I have explained earlier.

At the same time I must also take a hard look at the lifestyle that I myself and my friends adopt today. What I see is, once again, that morality runs throughout the aesthetic attitude of the Japanese.

Historically, when a samurai warrior died, "purity" was the foremost criterion. In this context purity refers to the removal of all moral defilement in preparation for a death of aesthetic propriety. This aesthetic beauty, however, is not man-made as in the West. Rather, it is a beauty which emphasizes oneness with nature, a beauty which does not detract from communion with nature.

花」という風景にシンボライズされることになります。そして、それはcleanな感覚を持っています。ふだんは隠されていますが、今日の生活の中にも、日本人はこのような生活の理想を求めつづけているといえると思います。

　実は、最近日本的経営として騒がれている工場管理・品質管理（QC）などは、このクリーン志向として古くからあったものです。人間関係も西欧的に近代化されたとはいえ、心底にはこの自然の秩序・調和に同化したいという傾向が生きています。

▶「あるべきようは」　これまでも何度か紹介した、樹の上で坐禅を組んでいた明恵上人（**図版㉙**）は、「あるべきようは」ということに、すべては尽きると言っています。

「人は、阿留辺幾夜宇和という七文字を持つべきなり。
　僧は僧のあるべきよう、俗は俗のあるべきようなり。
　乃至、帝王は帝王のあるべきよう、臣下は臣下のあるべきようなり。
　此のあるべきようを背く故に、一切悪きなり」

「あるべきようは」と言いますと、何もしないでいい、そのままでいいというように消極的な意味にも取れますが、そうではありません。理想的な姿は人間の社会であ

In its most concise form, one might say that beauty of this kind is symbolized by the phrase "snow, moon and flowers" which I discussed at the outset. These elements, this concept, are imbued with a sense of clean purity.

Today too, I believe, Japanese continue to seek after this same ideal in their daily lives, though it is not always obvious. Quality control in factories, for example—a topic given much publicity as a miracle of Japanese management—is really but a modern extension of an ancient affection for cleanliness.

Japanese human relations as well, despite their more recent "Westernization," are also fundamentally characterized by an inclination to strive for order and harmony with nature.

▶**Doing what comes naturally** Myoe, the Zen monk introduced earlier who was wont to meditate in trees (Fig. 29), said that everything has its own manner which is intrinsically and naturally proper:

> "Every man should be what he was meant to be.
> To the priest, there is a proper priestly way;
> To the layman, the proper way of laity.
> A lordly way for lords to be;
> A servile way for servants.
> To go against what is naturally proper
> Always leads to an evil end."

This exhortation to "do what comes naturally" might perhaps be taken as an enjoinment to do nothing, to stay with the status quo. But this is not what Myoe intended.

What he spoke of was an ideal, an ideal not determined by human society or an absolute god, but an ideal that is already demonstrated within the context of nature. In other words,

るとか、ある絶対的な神によって決められるものではない、それは、自然というものが、その現われの中ですでに規範を示している、したがって、自然の法則に従うことが最も理想的なあり方なのだということになります。

　明治以後の日本近代文学の代表者である夏目漱石（なつめそうせき）でさえ、彼の人生のモットーを〈則天去私（そくてんきょし）〉として掲げました。つまり、自我を去り、天の法則に合体せねばならないというのです。

　こういう考え方に対して、現代の日本人のビジネスマンの中には、そのような生き方では新しい発明や発見、技術革新はできないし、セールスもできない、つまり激しい国際的経営競争に負けてしまうと反論する人がいるのも事実です。

　しかしその意見は、前提になる自然というものを西欧的に動かないスタティックな素材と考えているからです。いま西欧でも、ニューサイエンティストと呼ばれる人々は、自然をトータルで調和のある機能的なストラクチャ（構造）、ダイナミックなプロセスと考えるようになりました。

▶「美的生き方」とは　では、どうすれば本来の自然に沿った生きかたができるのか、「あるべきようは」ということが実現されているか。これを判断するのは、私もきわめてエステティック（美的）な直感に頼っていると言わざるをえません。

obeyance of the laws of nature is the proper way to live.

Even Natsume Soseki (1867-1916), one of Japan's most famed writers of the modern period, expounded this philosophy by adopting the phrase *sokuten-kyoshi* as his life-long guiding principle: "Eradicate one's sense of self; follow the laws of nature."

Exhorting a modern-day Japanese businessman to follow the laws of nature, some would argue, is, for all its idealism, not very practical, as embracing such a philosophy would make it impossible to be a good salesman, or to make new inventions, new discoveries, new technologies—capabilities without which the Japanese would be unable to survive fierce international competition.

However, this view is based on the premise that nature is something inanimate or static, as it is in the Western interpretation. But even in the West, today there are people referred to as "new scientists" who see nature as a totally harmonious, functional structure or a dynamic process.

▶**Aesthetic perfection** How then does one succeed in living according to these laws of nature, in other words, according to the "manner one was meant to live?" The answer, I must confess, is extremely intangible and I can only rely on my aesthetic intuition.

This is because life and death are judged according to their degree of aesthetic perfection. This has been the case both with the aristocracy dating to the days of *The Tale of Genji* as well as powerful politicians and business leaders.

At all times, beauty is recognized when a person is in total harmony with the laws of nature. Acts of evil or impropriety are defilement and shame. In short, life and death are measured against the yardstick of nature, and anything deemed

なぜなら、平安時代の『源氏物語』でも、最も権力のある政治家や実業家の評価の際でも、その生き方・死に方が、いかに美的に完成されているかによって判断されていると言わざるをえないからです。

　つまり、自然の法則に人間が一致しているときは美しいと感じる、ですから醜い行動は穢れであり恥である。つまり自然に照らし合わせて、不自然であるというのが判断の基準になるわけです。

　これは倫理というよりも、きわめて感覚的なものなので、外国人には理解しがたいところがあるかもしれません。日本人としては、この感覚的なものを倫理としてわかりやすく構築しなおす必要があると思います。

▶世界の中の日本　さて結論として、今日はクロスカルチャー・文化交流の時代と言われますが、それはけっして文化を均質化することではなく、また、どちらをよしとし、どちらか悪いと判断することでもありません。それぞれの特殊性をよりよく理解することによって、初めて誤解がなくなり、差違を理解したうえに、より高い次元での共感の場が成り立つのではないでしょうか。

　日本は特殊な文化の国ではありますが、特殊性に引きこもったり、あるいは全面否定することは間違っています。特殊性を保ちながらインターナショナルを超えて、ユニバーサルな相互理解と人類の発展のために、世界文化に一つの刺激を与えることができるのではないかと思

"unnatural" is cause for criticism.

This concept is extremely intuitive rather than moralistic, and it may therefore be somewhat difficult for the non-Japanese to fully understand. As a Japanese, I believe it is necessary to take this intuitive concept and restructure it in more understandable, moralistic terms.

▶**Japan's role in the world**　We are said today to be in an age of cross-cultural exchange. This does not mean that all cultures should be "homogenized" or that some cultures should be judged better than others. Instead, cross-cultural exchange is an opportunity to better understand the distinctive differences of other cultures in order to eliminate misunderstanding.

Only through understanding on a higher plane such as this can we create an environment for mutual sympathy.

Japan is a nation with a unique culture. However, to withdraw into this uniqueness, or attempt to deny this uniqueness, would be wrong. Instead our role as Japanese, I would suggest, should be, while still maintaining our uniqueness, to provide a stimulus not merely for an "international" culture but for a *universal* culture, in order to achieve universal human understanding for the good of mankind and its development.

います。

▶**東洋的発想の重要性**　ただ、日本人はあまりにも日本という国を特殊に考えているかもしれません。日本とアメリカ、日本とヨーロッパという見方が、近代以来、ひじょうに強かった。しかし、日本はアジアの中の日本であり、東南アジアや中国、インド、韓国と文化的にも共通の地盤を持っているわけであります。

　点と点として、日本と西洋を鋭く対比するのではなくて、文化というものを、むしろ輪郭のぼやけた相互に重なり合う面と面として、世界的な文化の交流を考えていくべきだと思います。

　特に最近は、西欧近代産業主義が、行きづまりに来ています。このあまりにも巨大化し、人間のコントロールを越えて自己増殖する産業資本を、どうやって人間的なスケールに取り込み、伝統的なストラクチュアとして組み込むかという課題に戸惑い、その解答を出すのに、たいへん苦心をしています。

　このようなときに、今までのヨーロッパで発達した近代産業主義を補い改善するものとして、日本の、あるいはアジアの、自然に対する発想、自然との調和という考えが、新しい局面を開く手がかりになるかもしれません。

▶**日本人は残酷か**　一例として挙げますと、日本人の漁

▶**The importance of the Oriental system** Unfortunately, the Japanese see themselves, perhaps excessively, as a culture which is wholly unique. And this is understandable in view of the fact that there has been a strong tendency, especially in recent years, to think of Japan in comparative terms with the United States or Europe.

But Japan is, after all, an inherent part of Asia and it shares many cultural legacies with Southeast Asia, China, India and Korea. Rather than comparing cultures in terms of individual points—East vs. West, Japan vs. the West—I believe we should make comparisons in terms of broad regions, regions of blurred outline and overlapping borders. This, I suggest, is how we should consider "cultural exchanges" on a global scale.

Modern Western industrialism today has reached an impasse, having grown to monstrous proportions, self-propagating beyond human control. In consequence, man is now at a great loss how to bring it back to human scale and fit it back into the traditional structure system.

It is at a time such as this, perhaps, that Western industrialism as it developed in Europe can be repaired through an infusion of the Japanese or Asian philosophy toward nature and the necessity of living in harmony with nature. This infusion may provide just the breakthrough that is needed.

民がイルカを撲殺するのは、ひじょうに残酷だという抗議を、イギリスから受けたことがあります。また、このごろは聞きませんけれども、欧米人の間には、日本人は、刺身として、魚を生のまま食べるから、ひじょうに野蛮だという考え方もあるといいます。これを聞いたとき、日本とヨーロッパとの考え方の違いを痛感したのです。

　つまり、ヨーロッパ文明は、人間と動物をまったく違ったもの、初めから神の秩序によってその役割が定められたものと考えています。しかし、日本人の神道、あるいは仏教では、人間も来世では魚になったり、牛になったり、さまざまのものにメタモルフォーズ（転生）することもある、だから人間も魚も同じなんだと、同じレベルで考えます。

▶**放生会という儀式**　その一方で、日本には古くから生き物との調和と心の交流を確かめる儀式があることは、意外に知られていません。それは「供養」とか「放生会」といわれ、捕えられた魚や生き物を、生きたまま海や野原に戻してやることで、それまで犠牲になって死んでいった動物たちに感謝し、心を慰め、輪廻転生を確かめるという儀式です。

　このように日本人が自然との共感を示す対象は、単に動物にとどまりません。たとえば「針供養」というものがあります。お裁縫のときに使う針がたいへん疲れただ

▶**Japanese are cruel?** By way of example, Japanese fishermen were severely criticized in the U.K. several years ago for clubbing dolphins to death, falling under charges of excessive cruelty to these animals. Until quite recently the Japanese were also often censured by Westerners for their "barbaric" habit of eating raw fish. Incidents such as these made me realize quite deeply just how different are the views of Europe and Japan.

European civilization draws a clear demarcation between mankind and animals, each having set roles determined by divine providence. Japan, on the other hand, because of its Shinto and Buddhist influences believes that mankind at times undergoes metamorphosis and posthumously assumes another form of life, as a fish or a cow. Accordingly, men and fish are the same, and they are evaluated on the same level.

▶**A ritual of appeasement** It is true that the Japanese slaughter fish and eat it raw. But what is little known is that there is a certain ritual performed to confirm the spiritual relationship between man and other living creatures, in this case fish.

This ritual, known in Japanese as *kuyo* or *hojoe*, involves the release of some of the creatures captured alive, fish or whatever, back into their natural habitat—sea, prairie and so forth—and the offering of gratitude for those that have given their lives, along with prayers for their rebirth in the Buddhist cycle of transmigration.

This communion or sympathy with nature is manifested not only for living creatures like animals but even for inanimate objects such as sewing needles. Once each year women gather to perform a corresponding ritual to offer solace to sewing needles that have outlived their usefulness. The used needles

ろうということで婦人たちが集まって、1年に1回、豆腐という、ひじょうにやわらかい食べものに、折れた針を差してやって慰めるというものです。

▶**自然と動物と人間**　こういった自然観は、日本だけではなく、東洋全般に見られます。特にインドなどを旅行しますと、鳥が飛んできて人間のレストランの食事をついばんでいたり、あるいは牛が悠々と道を歩いているというような光景と出会います。自然と動物と人間が、同じレベルで一つの同じ自然のリサーキュレーション（循環）の中に組み込まれているということを強く感じます。

　まさに共生です。フランスの外交官で、中国・日本を深く愛したカトリック詩人・ポール・クローデルは、真の認識＝connaître（コネイトル）とは、co＝共に、naître＝生まれる、つまりともにひとつの関係に、ともに生きることにあると言っています。認識するものと、されるものという古典的な考え方はもう通用しません。ハイゼンベルクは量子力学の思想として、観察者が被観察者に力を及ぼす以上、その関係は一方的ではなく、ともにひとつの相関関係を作ることだと言っています。

　重ねて申しますが、これは日本と西欧とどちらがよく、どちらが悪いということではありません。図式的な対比だけが近代的で論理的だとはいえません。少なくとも現実的ではないでしょう。さまざまな異なった伝統的

are set upright in slabs of tofu, an extremely soft beancurd, as a sort of consolation or final resting place.

▶ **All on equal par**   This attitude toward nature is found not only in Japan but throughout most of the Orient. In India, for example, it is not uncommon to see birds being allowed to nibble at a patron's meal in a restaurant or cows walking boldly down the middle of the road.

This is because nature, animals and man are all taken as parts of the same structure, all on equal par, within the framework of a natural cycle of "recirculation."

What this amounts to is a form of symbiosis. Paul Claudel (1868-1955), the French Catholic poet and diplomat who deeply loved both Japan and China, once described true understanding by analyzing the word *connaître* (to know or understand) as *co* (together)+*naître* (be born), in other words sharing one life.

The classical view, which sees those in the "active" understanding role inherently separate from those placed in the "passive" understood role, no longer holds.

Werner Heisenberg (1901-76), the German physicist, proposed in his theories on quantum mechanics that the observer exerts an influence on the observed and therefore the relationship between the two is not uni-directional but interrelational.

Once again, I do not mean to imply in any way that one side, Japan or the West, is better or worse than the other. Schematic comparisons are not the only modern and logical approaches. If nothing else, they are not necessarily realistic. It is also necessary to stay keenly aware of the fact that numerous different cultural viewpoints lie at the base of mankind's political and economic institutions.

な考え方が、人類の政治や経済の制度（institute）の底に流れているんだということを、深く認識する必要があるということです。

▶雪月花の風景　日本の2000年に近い歴史を、わずかな言葉でお話しましたので、たいへん簡単なピックアップになりましたが、「雪月花」という三つのものが象徴する風景というものを、まず外国のみなさんにお贈りしたいと思います。

　折があって、みなさんが日本の風俗を見たり、政治や経済のミーティングをしたり、あるいは製品のデザインをごらんになるときには、この「雪月花」というシンボルを思い出していただきたい。ということは、目に見えるものよりも、その奥に真実がある、それも何か固いものではなくて、フレキシブル（柔軟）なシステムとしてそういうものをとらえているということです。

　このような見方を、一つのチャンネルとして、みなさんが覚えておいてくだされば、これから日本についてさまざまな疑問や不満をお感じになったときに、一つのキーワードとして使っていただけるでしょう。

　では、この日本文化の特質についてのお話を終わりたいと思います。

▶**The view of "setsu-getsu-ka"** I have discussed nearly 2,000 years of Japanese history in a very short time and have been able to touch only on a limited and random selection of topics. What I hope that I have done is given the foreign audience an appreciation of the Japanese concept of "snow, moon and flowers" and its historical role in Japanese culture.

In the future, when you come in contact with Japanese customs, when you look at a product of Japanese design, or when you take part in a political or economic meeting with Japanese, I hope that you will think back on snow, moon and flowers and will be reminded not to look merely on the surface but to search for the deeper truths that are always lying beneath.

There you may well discover the key that will open the door to a true understanding of Japan, harboring fewer suspicions and fewer dissatisfactions.

図版掲載作品・解説

1　富士曼荼羅図

富士山本宮浅間大社　静岡県富士宮市　**16 世紀**

たて 180cm ×横 118cm

古来、数多く描かれた富士山の中でも、最高傑作の一つに挙げられる名品。画面中央の浅間大社を中心とする富士参詣の曼荼羅で、山腹の左右に日月（太陽と月）を描き、敬虔な富士山浄土を表している。

2　紅白梅図屏風　尾形光琳筆

MOA 美術館　静岡県熱海市　**18 世紀　国宝**

二曲一双屏風　各・たて 156.5cm ×横 172.5cm

江戸時代前期の画壇を代表する巨匠・光琳（1658-1716）の最高傑作。その最晩年、58 歳ごろの作品。

3　山越阿弥陀図

禅林寺　京都市左京区　**13 世紀　国宝**

たて 138.0cm ×横 117.7cm

死者を阿弥陀仏が迎えにくるという、当時流行した阿弥陀来迎信仰に基づく作品。観音・勢至の両菩薩を先導に、いま山並みの上に、阿弥陀仏が半身を現したところ。

Detailed descriptions of all figures

1 "Fuji Mandala," 16th c.
Fuji Sengen Shrine, Fujinomiya, Shizuoka Pref.
H180×W118cm.
Considered among the great masterpieces depicting Mt. Fuji, this mandala shows the approach to the mountain passing through Sengen Shrine. The sun and moon seen on opposite sides near the mountain base serve as symbols of the sacred nature of this venerated peak.

2 "Red and White Plum Blossoms," by Ogata Korin, 18th c., National Treasure
MOA Museum of Art, Atami, Shizuoka Pref.
Pair of 2-fold screens, each H156.5×W172.5cm.
Ogata Korin (1658-1716) was one of the foremost artists of the early Edo period. These highly treasured screen paintings are among his last works.

3 "Amitabha Crossing the Mountains," 13th c., National Treasure
Zenrinji Temple, Sakyo-ku, Kyoto
H138.0×W117.7cm.
Founded on the popular belief that Amitabha comes to escort the deceased, this painting describes his approach over a mountain ridge. The bodhisattvas Kannon (Avalokiteśvara) and Seishi (Mahāsthāmaprāpta) welcome him.

4 富嶽三十六景　神奈川沖浪裏　葛飾北斎筆

東京国立博物館　19世紀

たて 26.4cm ×横 38.0cm

安藤広重と並ぶ風景版画の第一人者・北斎（1760-1849）の代表作。逆巻く波と小舟の上にひれ伏す人々、その向こう側に富士。構図の大胆さ、静と動の対比が見事。

5 高雄観楓図　狩野秀頼筆

東京国立博物館　16世紀　国宝

六曲屏風一隻　たて 149.1cm ×横 363.9cm

16、17世紀に盛んに描かれた風俗画の代表作。京都北部、高雄山の紅葉のもとで遊楽している様を表している。

6 凍雲篩雪図　浦上玉堂筆

川端康成記念会　神奈川県鎌倉市　19世紀　国宝

たて 133.5cm ×横 56.2cm

玉堂（1745-1820）は、50歳で脱藩。以後、放浪の旅を続けた異色の文人画家。本図は、冬枯れの凍てつくような自然の情景を描いたもの。

4 "Fuji through the Waves," from "Thirty-six Views of Mt. Fuji," by Katsushika Hokusai, 19th c.

Tokyo National Museum
H26.4×W38.0cm.

This woodblock print, showing Mt. Fuji as seen from offshore in Kanagawa, ranks among the most famous works of Katsushika Hokusai (1760-1849), who, along with Ando Hiroshige, took landscape painting to new heights during the Edo period. The work is particularly remarkable for its boldness of composition and contrast between movement and serenity.

5 "Maple Viewing at Takao," by Kano Hideyori, 16th c., National Treasure

Tokyo National Museum
H149.1×W363.9cm.

This screen portraying an excursion to view maple foliage at Mt. Takao north of Kyoto is a representative work of genre painting popular during the 16th and 17th centuries.

6 "Landscape in Snow," by Uragami Gyokudo, 19th c., National Treasure

Kawabata Foundation, Kamakura
H133.5×W56.2cm.

Uragami Gyokudo (1745-1820) was an unusual artist who abandoned his feudal domain at the age of 50 to begin a life of wandering. This painting vividly describes the frigid beauty of nature in winter.

7 洛中洛外図巻　住吉具慶筆

東京国立博物館　**17世紀**

たて 40.9cm ×横 1368.0cm

具慶（1631-1705）は、住吉派の祖である如慶の子。宮中で活躍したのち、江戸にやまと絵の美意識を持ち込んだ。

8 縄文式土器　火炎型土器A式2号

長岡市立科学博物館　新潟県　**縄文時代中期**

高さ 32cm

長岡市内の馬高遺跡から出土した。

9 色絵藤花文茶壺　野々村仁清作

MOA美術館　静岡県熱海市　**17世紀　国宝**

高さ 28.8cm

江戸時代初期の陶工・仁清（生没年不詳）の代表作。形成の精巧さ、金銀五彩を施した鮮麗な色絵付など、縄文・弥生から続く日本の壺においても最高傑作。

10 正殿

伊勢神宮内宮　三重県伊勢市

棟高 10.3m

20年ごとに造替を繰り返す。現在の建物は、1993年、61回目の遷宮によるもの。

7 "Scenes In and Around Kyoto," painted scroll, 17th c.
Tokyo National Museum
H40.9×W1368.0cm
Sumiyoshi Gukei (1631-1705) was the son of Jokei, founder of the Sumiyoshi school of painting. Initially active in court circles in Kyoto, he advanced the embracement of the Yamato-e painting style in Edo (Tokyo).

8 "Flame-style Earthenware Type A, Number 2,"
Middle Jomon period (3000-2000B.C.)
Nagaoka Municipal Science Museum, Nagaoka, Niigata Pref.
Height: 32cm.
Provenance: Umataka

9 **Tea Jar with Wisteria Design,** by Nonomura Ninsei, 17th c., National Treasure
MOA Museum of Art, Atami, Shizuoka Pref.
Height: 28.8cm.
This exquisitely shaped jar, featuring elaborate painting in brilliant colors with gold and silver trim, continues in the tradition of Jomon and Yayoi styles. A representative work of Ninsei (fl. late 17th c.), it is prized as one of Japan's finest ceramic jars.

10 Main Sanctuary
Ise Shrine, Ise, Mie Pref.
Height: 10.3m.
Since ancient times, the Ise Shrine has been completely reconstructed every 20 years. The present structure, dating to 1993, represents the sixty-first rebuilding.

11　本殿
出雲大社　島根県出雲市　**1744 年造替　国宝**
棟高約 24m
その巨大さは、強力な神威を表す。

12　五重塔と金堂
法隆寺　奈良県斑鳩町　**7 世紀　国宝**
五重塔・高さ 34.1m　金堂・高さ 16.4m
世界最古の木造建築群。

13　金堂壁画
法隆寺　奈良県斑鳩町　**7 世紀**（1949 年焼失）
インド的要素が濃厚な作品。中国にもほとんど類例がなく、焼失が惜しまれて余りある。現在は、模写が堂内に掲げられている。

14　菩薩半跏像
中宮寺　奈良県斑鳩町　**7 世紀　国宝**
像高 133.0cm　木造
黒光りして一見ブロンズのようだが、クス材からなる木彫の名作である。

15　聖観音像
薬師寺東院堂　奈良市　**8 世紀　国宝**
像高 188.9cm　銅造
胸もとや腰に垂らした装飾具が、この像をいっそう華やかにしている。

11 Main Sanctuary, Izumo Shrine, reconstructed 1744, National Treasure
Izumo, Shimane Pref.
Height: approx. 24m.
The shrine's imposing scale evokes the power of the Shinto deities.

12 Five-storied Pagoda and Kondo Hall, 7th c., National Treasures
Horyuji Temple, Ikaruga, Nara Pref.
Pagoda height: 34.1m. Kondo height: 16.4m.
The temple complex at Horyuji contains the oldest wooden structures in the world.

13 Wall Painting of Kondo, 7th c. (lost to fire, 1949)
Horyuji Temple, Ikaruga, Nara Pref.
The loss of this rare painting, particularly prized for its strong Indian influences, is painfully regrettable. Even in China there are but few works of similar nature. Today a copy of the original is on display in the Kondo.

14 Seated Bodhisattva, 7th c., National Treasure
Chuguji Temple, Ikaruga, Nara Pref.
Wood. Height: 133.0cm.
Although its black luster gives the visual impression of cast bronze, this extremely prized statue is actually carved from camphor wood.

15 Sho Kannon Bodhisattva, 8th c., National Treasure
Toin-do (East Hall), Yakushiji Temple, Nara
Bronze. Height: 188.9cm.
The decorative ornaments pendant from the neck and waist add to the statue's resplendent beauty.

16 東塔(とうとう)

薬師寺　奈良市　8世紀　国宝

高さ約34m

フェノロサによって「凍(こお)れる音楽」と評された天平建築の代表。

17 投入堂(なげいれ)

三仏寺奥院　鳥取県三朝町　11世紀　国宝

険しい山道の先に建てられ、修験の霊場としてあがめられてきた。堂内に蔵王権現(ざおうごんげん)をまつっている。

18 大日如来(だいにちによらい)　運慶(うんけい)作

円成寺　奈良市　1176年　国宝

像高98.8cm　木造

現存する運慶の作品は20件に及ぶともいわれるが、本像は最も古く、彼が20代のときに制作された。若い感性がほとばしっている。

19 十一面観音像

向源寺　滋賀県高月町　9世紀　国宝

像高194.0cm　木造

琵琶湖東北岸の寺・向源寺の本尊。引きしまった目鼻立ちには生気がみなぎり、腰をひねり、片膝をゆるめて立つポーズには、独特の流動感がある。

16 **Three-storied Pagoda,** 8th c., National Treasure
Yakushiji Temple, Nara
Height: approx. 34m.
A representative structure of the Tempyo era, this pagoda inspired famed art historian Ernest Fenollosa (1853-1908) to describe it as "frozen music."

17 **Nageiredo,** 11th c., National Treasure
Sanbutsuji Temple, Misasa-cho, Tottori Pref.
Built into a precipice at the end of a steep mountain path, the Nageiredo has long been a holy site to Shugendo mountain worshipers. The structure originally contained statues of the deity Zao Gongen.

18 **Dainichi-nyorai (Mahāvairocana),** 1176, National Treasure
Enjoji Temple, Nara
Wood. Height: 98.8cm.
This statue is said to be the oldest of 20 surviving works by the renowned sculptor Unkei (?-1223). Created when he was in his twenties, it reflects his youthful sensibilities.

19 **Juichimen Kannon,** 9th c., National Treasure
Kogenji Temple, Takatsuki, Shiga Pref.
Wood. Height: 194.0cm.
This statue serves as the main icon of Kogenji, a Buddhist temple located on the northeastern shore of Lake Biwa.

20 清涼殿(せいりょうでん)

京都御所　京都市上京区

棟高 14.1m

これは、かつての天皇たちが日常生活を送った建物である。

21 海に浮かぶ神社

厳島神社　広島県廿日市市　12世紀造営　国宝

鳥居の高さ　約 16m

海の中の鳥居が目を奪う。現在の社殿は、鎌倉・室町期のもの。

22 鳳凰堂(ほうおう)

平等院　京都府宇治市　11世紀　国宝

棟高 16.3m

楼閣(ろうかく)形式の本堂、堂内の仏像と荘厳、本堂前面の池……。「地上の極楽浄土」に不可欠なすべての要素が現存する貴重な作例。

23 鳳凰堂内部

平等院　京都府宇治市　11世紀　国宝

壁面には雲の中を飛びまわる小さな菩薩像が多数かけられ、壁画も描かれている。阿弥陀仏の光背(こうはい)、天蓋(てんがい)(吊り天井)の装飾も豪華を極め、この世の浄土を表現している。

20 Kyoto Imperial Palace (Seiryoden Hall)
Kamigyo-ku, Kyoto
Height: 14.1m.
This building originally served as the living quarters of successive Emperors.

21 Floating Shrine, orig. 12th c,. National Treasure
Itsukushima Shrine, Hatsukaichi, Hiroshima Pref.
The "floating" torii gate (height: approx. 16m) of Itsukushima Shrine is one of Japan's most beautiful and deservedly famed sights. The shrine's existing structure dates to the Kamakura and Muromachi periods.

22 Hoo-do (Phoenix Hall), 11th c., National Treasure
Byodoin Temple, Uji, Kyoto Pref.
Height: 16.3m.
With its palatial main hall, exquisite Buddhist statues and ornate decoration adorning its interior, and pristine pond in its foreground, Byodoin is a rare surviving example of a temple containing all the elements indispensable to "Paradise on Earth."

23 Interior of Hoo-do (Phoenix Hall)
The interior walls of Byodoin's Phoenix Hall are decorated with numerous small wooden figurines of bodhisattvas engaged in various pursuits on beds of clouds. Below them are a wealth of religious murals. The exceptionally ornate nimbus and canopy of the Amida Buddha symbolize the Pure Land on earth.

24　源氏物語絵巻　柏木(かしわぎ)

徳川美術館　名古屋市　12 世紀　国宝

たて 22cm

本図は、光源氏の怒りを買い、死期の近い柏木を、旧友であり源氏の息子でもある夕霧(ゆうぎり)が見舞う場面。

25　鳥獣人物戯画

高山寺　京都市右京区　12 世紀　国宝

全四巻の甲巻・各巻・たて 31cm 全長 10m 前後

鳥獣を擬人化して遊戯や行事を描く。軽快でユーモラスな画面展開だが、当時の仏教界や世相を、巧みに風刺している。

26　三十六人家(か)集　能宣(よしのぶ)集

西本願寺　京都市下京区　12 世紀　国宝

たて 19.9cm

宮中に長く伝えられたが、1549 年、後奈良(こなら)天皇から本願寺十世証如(しょうにょ)に贈られた。

27　扇面法華経冊子(せんめんほけきょうさっし)　巻第一

四天王寺　大阪市　12 世紀　国宝

たて 25.6cm

物語に耳を傾ける少女の表情が愛らしい。それにしても、なんとすばらしい光景だろう。

24 **Scene from *The Tale of Genji* Scrolls,** 12th c., National Treasure
Tokugawa Art Museum, Nagoya
Height: 22cm.
In this scene, Yugiri, son of Genji, comes to visit his close friend Kashiwagi, who has incurred Genji's wrath and is now on his deathbed.

25 **Monochrome Animal Caricatures,** 12th c., National Treasure
Kozanji Temple, Ukyo-ku, Kyoto
Part of set of 4 scrolls, each approx. 31cm high and 10m long. This satirical scroll is one of a series known as "Scrolls of Frolicking Animals and Humans" (*Choju jimbutsu giga*) that personify members of the animal kingdom to describe human entertainments and functions in a light, humorous vein. They cleverly poke fun at the Buddhist world and popular customs.

26 *Anthology of the Thirty-six Poets,* 12th c., National Treasure
Nishi-Honganji Temple, Shimogyo-ku, Kyoto
Height: 19.9cm.
Long passed down within the imperial court, in 1549 this anthology was presented by Emperor Gonara to Shonyo, the 10th Spiritual Leader of Honganji.

27 **Fan-shaped Album of the *Lotus Sutra*,** Volume 1, 12th c., National Treasure
Shitennoji Temple, Osaka
Height: 25.6cm.
This magnificent work vividly depicts a young girl listening entranced to a story.

28 源頼朝像

神護寺　京都市右京区　12世紀　国宝

たて143.0cm×横112.8cm

筆者は藤原隆信（1142-1205）と伝えられる。日本の肖像画の代表作。

29 明恵上人像

高山寺　京都市右京区　13世紀　国宝

たて142.5cm×横58.8cm

山中で坐禅する明恵の像。弟子の成忍が師を偲んで描いたといわれる。

30 一遍上人絵伝

東京国立博物館　13世紀　国宝

全十二巻のうちの巻七　たて38.2cm

日本中を旅する一遍は、いよいよ京都に入り、念仏踊を勧進する。

31 千体千手観音像

妙法院三十三間堂　京都市東山区　13世紀　国宝

像高　約166cm

内陣の柱間が三十三間、約118mの堂内に一千一体の千手観音が立ち並ぶ様は壮観。

28 Portrait of Minamoto no Yoritomo, 12th c., National Treasure
Jingoji Temple, Ukyo-ku, Kyoto
H143.0×W112.8cm.
Attributed to the brush of Fujiwara no Takanobu (1142-1205), this highly prized work ranks among Japan's foremost portrait paintings.

29 Portrait of Monk Myoe, 13th c., National Treasure
Kozanji Temple, Ukyo-ku, Kyoto
H142.5×58.8cm.
This well-known portrait of Myoe, showing him deep in meditation, is believed to have been drawn by his disciple Jonin in his master's memory.

30 Painted Scroll from "A Pictorial Biography of Monk Ippen," 13th c., National Treasure
Tokyo National Museum
Seventh of 12 scrolls. Height: 38.2cm.
Ippen, an itinerant monk whose travels took him all around the Japanese archipelago, is shown at a temple in Kyoto where he leads the faithful in a "dance of intonement."

31 Thousand Statues of Senju Kannon, 13th c., National Treasure
Sanjusangendo Hall, Myohoin Temple, Higashiyama-ku, Kyoto
The Sanjusangen Hall, named for its inner sanctum of 33 (*sanjusan*) bays (*ken*) stretching approximately 118 meters, contains the imposing sight of 1,001 statues of the "thousand-armed" Kannon.

32 金閣と庭園
鹿苑寺　京都市北区　**14世紀創建　特別名勝**
足利義満の建立。金閣は、1950年に焼失、1955年に再建された。

33 銀閣
慈照寺　京都市左京区　**15世紀　国宝**
棟高 10.8m
もとは足利義政の別荘・東山殿(ひがしやまどの)。

34 洪隠山石組(こういんざん)
西芳寺　京都市右京区　**14世紀　特別名勝**
一流の庭師は、石に生命を吹き込んで据(す)える。

35 枯山水庭園
大仙院　京都市北区　**16世紀　特別名勝**
庭の中にある大小すべての石に名前がつけられている。

36 天橋立図(あまのはしだて)　雪舟筆(せっしゅう)
京都国立博物館　**16世紀　国宝**
たて 89.5cm ×横 169.5cm
画聖雪舟（1420-1506）最晩年の傑作とされるが、制作の経緯はよくわかっていない。実景の写しと精神的な心象が高い次元で結びついている。

32 Kinkaku (Golden Pavilion), orig. 14th c., Special Place of Scenic Beauty
Rokuonji Temple, Kita-ku, Kyoto
Originally constructed under Ashikaga Yoshimitsu in the 14th century, the famed Golden Pavilion was rebuilt in 1955 after being destroyed by fire in 1950.

33 Ginkaku (Silver Pavilion), 15th c., National Treasure
Jishoji Temple, Sakyo-ku, Kyoto
Height: 10.8m.
The so-called Silver Pavilion was built as a villa for Ashikaga Yoshimasa in the Higashiyama area of Kyoto.

34 "Koinzan" Rock Formation, 14th c., Special Place of Scenic Beauty
Saihoji Temple, Ukyo-ku, Kyoto
The landscape gardener has applied his supreme skills to breathe life into the thoughtfully placed rocks.

35 Stone Garden, 16th c., Special Place of Scenic Beauty
Daisen-in Monastery, Daitokuji Temple, Kita-ku, Kyoto
All rocks in this garden, both large and small, have designated names.

36 "View of Amanohashidate," by Sesshu, 16th c., National Treasure
Kyoto National Museum
H89.5×W169.5cm.
This masterpiece by Sesshu (1420-1506) is said to have been painted late in his life, but the details behind its creation are unknown. It brilliantly combines a depiction of real scenery with the artist's mental imagery.

37　那智滝図

根津美術館　東京都　13世紀　国宝

たて159.1cm×横58.0cm

和歌山県南部の那智滝は、古くから信仰の対象として崇敬されてきた。本図は、きわめて写実的な描法を用いつつ、宗教的雰囲気をも描き出している。

38　能面　孫次郎

三井記念美術館　東京都　16世紀

面長21.2cm

能楽の金剛家に伝わった名品の一つ。孫次郎久次が、亡き妻の面影を偲んで作ったといわれている。

39　北能舞台

西本願寺　京都市下京区　16世紀　国宝

現存最古の能舞台。床下には、音響効果を高めるための甕がおかれている。

40　檜図屛風　狩野永徳筆

東京国立博物館　16世紀　国宝

たて169.7cm×横460.5cm

檜の巨木が画面いっぱいに枝を伸ばす。充満する旺盛な生命感が、戦国大名の活躍した桃山時代の空気を伝える。

37 "Nachi Waterfall," 13th c., National Treasure
Nezu Art Museum, Tokyo
H159.1×W58.0cm.
Nachi Waterfall, located in southern Wakayama Prefecture, has long been worshiped as a symbol of Shinto faith. This painting brilliantly evokes a religious mood even as it relies on the use of realism.

38 "Magojiro" Noh Mask, 16th c.
Mitsui Memorial Museum, Tokyo
Length: 21.2cm.
This Noh mask of a young woman is said to have been created by Magojiro Hisatsugu in memory of his late wife. It has been passed down through generations of the Kongo school.

39 North Noh Stage, 16th c., National Treasure
Nishi-Honganji Temple, Shimogyo-ku, Kyoto
This is the oldest extant Noh stage in Japan. Ceramic jars are strategically placed beneath the floorboards to heighten the acoustic effects.

40 "Japanese Cypress," by Kano Eitoku, 16th c., National Treasure
Tokyo National Museum
H169.7×W460.5cm.
This giant cypress tree, its trunk and branches dynamically spreading to all corners of the canvas, conveys the energetic mood of the Momoyama period, an age of feudal warlords vying for supremacy.

41 天守

松本城　長野県松本市　16世紀　国宝

棟高 25m

姫路城（兵庫県）、彦根城（滋賀県）などとともに、創建当初の姿を今に伝える数少ない遺構の一つ。古いばかりでなく、姿の秀麗さでも特筆に価(あたい)する。

42 待庵(たいあん)内部

妙喜庵　京都府大山崎町　16世紀　国宝

千利休作の茶室として現存する唯一の例。一切の装飾を排除し、簡素の美を追求した草庵風茶室の代表。

43 志野(しの)茶碗　銘「卯花墻(うのはながき)」

三井記念美術館　東京都　16世紀　国宝

高さ 9.6cm

国産茶陶の白眉(はくび)。

44 黒楽(くろらく)茶碗　銘「あやめ」　長次郎(ちょうじろう)作

MOA美術館　静岡県熱海市　16世紀

高さ 8.9cm

長次郎（1516-92年）は、千利休の侘(わ)茶精神に適する茶碗を作った陶工。手で捏(こ)ねて成形し、低火度で焼き上げ、量感のある渋い色あいが特徴。

41 **Matsumoto Castle,** 16th C., National Treasure
Matsumoto, Nagano Pref.
Height: 25m.
Matsumoto Castle is a rare architectural specimen which, like Himeji (Hyogo Pref.) and Hikone (Shiga Pref.) Castles, survives as a living monument of the age of its construction. The castle is prized not only for its antiquity but also for its graceful beauty.

42 **Interior of Taian Teahouse,** 16th c., National Treasure
Oyamazaki, Kyoto Pref.
This bare and simple structure is the only extant example of a teahouse designed by the great tea master Sen no Rikyu. It is representative of the so-called "thatched hermitage" (*soan*) type of teahouse created in pursuit of unadorned simplicity.

43 **"Unohanagaki" Shino Style Tea Bowl,** 16th c., National Treasure
Mitsui Memorial Museum, Tokyo
Height: 9.6cm.
This is one of Japan's most outstanding examples of locally produced tea ceramics.

44 **"Ayame" Raku Ware Tea Bowl,** by Chojiro, 16th c.
MOA Museum of Art, Atami, Shizuoka Pref.
Height: 8.95cm.
Chojiro (1516-92) was a potter who made tea bowls in keeping with the austere spirit of Sen no Rikyu. Each bowl was shaped by hand and low-fired to produce a beautifully tactile, weighty character.

45 伊賀水指　銘「破袋」
五島美術館　東京都　16世紀
高さ 8.9cm
大きなひび割れが茶人たちによって賞賛されてきた。

46　花入　銘「園城寺」　千利休作
東京国立博物館　16世紀
高さ 33.9cm
小田原遠征に同行した利休が、当地で秀吉に献じた。表面のひび割れを園城寺にある有名な割れ鐘になぞらえて、命名された。

47　陽明門
東照宮　栃木県日光市　17世紀　国宝
棟高 11.1m
徳川将軍家の廟所として造営された東照宮。華麗な装飾建築の代表。

48　書院
桂離宮　京都市右京区　17世紀
同時代の東照宮と対照的に、簡素な書院造の代表建築。

45 "Yaburebukuro" Water Jar, Iga ware, 16th c.
Goto Art Museum, Tokyo
Height: 21cm.
Large cracks in ceramics have long been admired by connoisseurs of the tea ceremony.

46 "Onjoji" Flower Vase, 1590, by Sen no Rikyu
Tokyo National Museum
Bamboo. Height: 33.9cm.
This vase was presented by Sen no Rikyu to Toyotomi Hideyoshi (1537-98) during the "Odawara Campaign." Its name derives from the similarity of its surface cracks to those of a famed bell at Onjoji Temple.

47 Yomei Gate, 17th c., National Treasure
Toshogu Shrine, Nikko, Tochigi Pref.
Height: 11.1m.
Toshogu Shrine was built as a mausoleum for leaders of the Tokugawa Shogunate. The Yomei Gate is renowned for its elaborate ornateness.

48 Katsura Detached Palace, 17th c.
Ukyo-ku, Kyoto
In contrast with Toshogu Shrine, a contemporary structure, the Katsura Detached Palace features the extremely simple *shoin-zukuri* style of residential architecture.

49　奥書院上段の間

金刀比羅宮　香川県琴平町　18世紀

伊藤若冲(じゃくちゅう)（1716-1800）の手による華麗な花丸(はなまる)図が、部屋一面を飾っている。

50　遊楽図屏風

徳川美術館　名古屋市　17世紀

八曲一双屏風のうち右隻　たて126.1cm×横407.8cm

屋外と屋内のさまざまな遊楽図。二階建ての豪壮な邸宅で、遊里の建物とその情景を理想化して描いている。

51　洛中洛外図(らくちゅうらくがい)　上杉本(うえすぎ)　狩野永徳筆

上杉美術館　山形県米沢市　16世紀　国宝

六曲一双屏風のうち右隻　たて160.4cm×横365.2cm

織田信長が上杉謙信に贈ったという由来を伝える。御所や祇(ぎ)園祭(おん)の山鉾(やまぼこ)、鴨川、金閣など、都の代表的景物が、2500人の人物とともに書き込まれている。

52　婦女遊楽図屏風（松浦(まつうら)屏風）

大和文華館　奈良市　17世紀　国宝

六曲一双屏風のうち左隻　たて153.0cm×横363.0cm

全面金地(きんじ)の上に、豪華な衣装を身に着けた遊里(ゆうり)の女性たちの姿態を描く。

49   Oku-shoin (Inner Drawing Room), 18th c.
Kotohiragu (Kompira) Shrine, Kotohira-cho, Kagawa Pref.
The room is completely decorated in elaborate flower paintings by Ito Jakuchu (1716-1800).

50   "Merriments," 17th c.
Tokugawa Art Museum, Nagoya
Right half of pair of 8-fold screens, each H126.1×W407.8cm. This genre painting shows the idealized entertainments of patrons of the gay quarters. The sumptuousness of the two-storied structure is especially remarkable.

51   "Scenes In and Around Kyoto" (Uesugi version), 16th c., by Kano Eitoku, National Treasure
Yonezawa City Uesugi Museum, Yamagata Pref.
Right half of pair of 6-fold screens, each H160.4×W365.2cm. These screens were a gift from Oda Nobunaga (1534-82) to the warlord Uesugi Kenshin (1530-78). In all, some 2,500 figures are depicted against the backdrop of sights representative of Kyoto, including the Imperial Palace, Kamo River and Golden Pavilion. Here we see the Gion Festival and its elaborate floats.

52   Genre Scene, 17th c., National Treasure
The Museum Yamatobunkakan, Nara
Left half of pair of 6-fold screens, each H153.0×W363.0cm. This scene portrays the subtle movements of the ladies of the demimonde against a background of plain gold. The richness and variety of their kimonos merit special attention.

53　十二ヶ月風俗図　十一月「御火焚(おひたき)」
山口蓬春記念館　神奈川県葉山町　**16世紀**

たて32.7cm×横28.0cm

火の粉を浴び、残り火で焼いた蜜柑(みかん)や餅を食べることで、子どもたちの無病息災を願った。

54　婦女風俗十二ヶ月図　勝川春章(かつかわしゅんしょう)筆
MOA美術館　静岡県熱海市　**18世紀**

たて94.0cm×横25.5cm

一年の各月の風物と、婦女を描いた連作。本図はそのうちの十二月、節分の図。

55　婦人相学十躰(ふじんそうがくじつたい)　浮気(うわき)の相　喜多川歌麿(うたまろ)筆
東京国立博物館　**18世紀**

たて38.7cm×横25.7cm

美人画の巨匠・歌麿（1753-1806年）の代表作。女性の細やかな仕草の表現が、そのまま心理描写にまで達している。

53 "Ohitaki Festival" (November), 16th c.
One of a series of 12 genre paintings (calendar).
Hoshun Yamaguchi Memorial Hall, Hayama-cho, Kanagawa Pref.
H32.7×W28.0cm.
By passing through a shower of sparks from a bonfire and eating mandarin oranges and rice cakes baked in the embers, prayers were offered for the health of children.

54 "Illustrations of the Twelve Months," by Katsukawa Shunsho, 18th c.
MOA Museum of Art, Atami, Shizuoka Pref.
H94.0×W25.5cm.
This is one of a series of paintings illustrating everyday customs observed by ladies during each month of the year.

55 "Coquettish Woman," by Kitagawa Utamaro, 18th c.
Tokyo National Museum
H38.7×W25.7cm.
One of a series of ten woodblock prints showing women representing different traits, this famed work by the great master Utamaro (1753-1806) is prized for the depth of its characterization that extends beyond the physical into the psychological.

写真借出先・撮影者（登場順）

富士山本宮浅間大社　1
MOA 美術館　2　9　**44**　**54**
禅林寺　3
TNM イメージアーカイブ　4　5　**7**　**30**　**40**　46　**55**
日本近代文学館　6
長岡市立科学博物館　**8**
伊勢神宮　**10**
出雲大社　**11**
飛鳥園　**12**　**13**　**14**　**15**　18
薬師寺　**16**
三仏寺　17
向源寺　19
宮内庁京都事務所　**20**　**48**
ニッショウプロ（富本淳司撮影）　**21**
平等院　**22**　**23**
徳川黎明会　**24**　**50**
京都国立博物館（金井杜道撮影）　25　**28**　**29**　**36**
西本願寺　**26**　**39**
四天王寺　**27**
妙法院　31
鹿苑寺（柴田秋介撮影）　**32**
慈照寺　**33**
井上博道　**34**
大仙院　**35**
根津美術館　37
三井記念美術館　**38**　**43**
松本城管理事務所　**41**
便利堂　**42**
五島美術館（名鏡勝朗撮影）　**45**
小学館　**47**
金刀比羅宮　49
二見興玉神社　p153
米沢市上杉博物館　**51**
大和文華館（入江宏太郎撮影）　**52**
JR 東海生涯学習財団　53

★読者のみなさまにお願い

この本をお読みになって、どんな感想をお持ちでしょうか。祥伝社のホームページから書評をお送りいただけたら、ありがたく存じます。今後の企画の参考にさせていただきます。また、次ページの原稿用紙を切り取り、左記まで郵送していただいても結構です。

お寄せいただいた書評は、ご了解のうえ新聞・雑誌などを通じて紹介させていただくこともあります。採用の場合は、特製図書カードを差しあげます。

なお、ご記入いただいたお名前、ご住所、ご連絡先等は、書評紹介の事前了解、謝礼のお届け以外の目的で利用することはありません。また、それらの情報を6カ月を越えて保管することもありません。

〒101-8701 (お手紙は郵便番号だけで届きます)

祥伝社　新書編集部

電話 03 (3265) 2310

祥伝社ブックレビュー　www.shodensha.co.jp/bookreview

★本書の購買動機（媒体名、あるいは○をつけてください）

＿＿＿新聞の広告を見て	＿＿＿誌の広告を見て	＿＿＿の書評を見て	＿＿＿のWebを見て	書店で見かけて	知人のすすめで

★100字書評……雪月花の心

名前
住所
年齢
職業

栗田　勇　（くりた・いさむ）

1926年、東京生まれ。東京大学仏文科卒業。フランス象徴主義の詩人・ロートレアモンの個人全訳（本邦初）を皮切りに、多彩な創作評論活動を展開。日本文化論の第一人者として知られる。1978年、『一遍上人』により芸術選奨文部大臣賞を受賞。著書には、『道元の読み方』『白隠禅師の読み方』『一休 その破戒と風狂』『千利休と日本人』（以上弊社刊）、『花を旅する』などがある。講談社から、全12巻の著作集を刊行した。1999年、紫綬褒章受章。2023年、逝去。

ロバート・ミンツァー（英訳）

1949年、アメリカ・ニュージャージー州生まれ。ハーバード大学院で日本古典文学を学び、博士号取得。1995年、日本に帰化、室生寺玲（むろうじ・れい）に改名する。

雪月花の心
せつげつか　こころ

栗田　勇
くりた　いさむ
ロバート・ミンツァー（英訳）

2008年11月 5 日　初版第 1 刷発行
2024年12月25日　　　第 2 刷発行

発行者	辻 浩明
発行所	祥伝社 しょうでんしゃ
	〒101-8701　東京都千代田区神田神保町3-6-5
	電話　03(3265)2081（販売）
	電話　03(3265)2310（編集）
	電話　03(3265)3622（製作）
	ホームページ　www.shodensha.co.jp
装丁者	盛川和洋
印刷所	萩原印刷
製本所	ナショナル製本

造本には十分注意しておりますが、万一、落丁、乱丁などの不良品がありましたら、「製作」あてにお送りください。送料小社負担にてお取り替えいたします。ただし、古書店で購入されたものについてはお取り替え出来ません。本書の無断複写は著作権法上での例外を除き禁じられています。また、代行業者など購入者以外の第三者による電子データ化及び電子書籍化は、たとえ個人や家庭内での利用でも著作権法違反です。

Printed in Japan ISBN978-4-396-11134-2 C0270

〈祥伝社新書〉
日本文化と美

201 日本文化のキーワード 七つのやまと言葉
あわれ、におい、わび・さび、道、間……七つの言葉から日本文化に迫る

作家 **栗田 勇**

413 思いがけない日本美術史
日本画はいつも新鮮！ 長谷川等伯、仙厓ら12の作品から知る鑑賞のツボ

明治神宮ミュージアム館長 **黒田泰三**

561 ゆるカワ日本美術史
土偶、埴輪から仏像、絵巻、禅画、近代絵画まで、kawaiiの源流を辿る

跡見学園女子大学教授 **矢島 新**

336 日本の10大庭園 何を見ればいいのか
龍安寺庭園、毛越寺庭園など10の名園を紹介。日本庭園の基本原則がわかる

作庭家 **重森千靑**

580 大伴旅人 人と作品
「令和」の生みの親である大伴旅人の生涯を四期に分け、歌と共に解説

国際日本文化研究センター名誉教授 **中西 進** 編